Your Joke Is in the E-Mail

(:))

Your Joke Is in the E-Mail

(Cyberlaffs from Mousepotatoes)

**Alice Kahn and
John Dobby Boe**

Ten Speed Press
Berkeley, California

Ten Speed Press
Box 7123
Berkeley, CA 94707

Distributed in Australia by Simon & Schuster Australia, in Canada by Publishers Group West, in New Zealand by Tandem Press, in South Africa by Real Books, in the United Kingdom and Europe by Airlift Books, and in Singapore, Malaysia, and Indonesia by Berkeley Books.

Cover design by Cale Burr

Interior design by Victor Ichioka

Library of Congress Cataloging-in-Publication Data

Your joke is in the e-mail : cyberlaffs from mousepotatoes /
[compiled] by Alice Kahn & John Dobby Boe.
        p.   cm.
    ISBN 0-89815-988-1
    1. Internet (Computer network)—humor. 2. Electronic mail systems —Quotations, maxims, etc. 3. Internet (Computer network)— Quotations, maxims, etc. 4. Electronic mail systems—Quotations, maxims, etc.
I. Kahn, Alice, 1943– . II. Boe, John, 1944– .
PN9231.I62Y68 1997
818'.540208—dc21   97-40737
                                                      CIP

First printing, 1997

Printed in Canada

1 2 3 4 5 6 7 8 9 10 — 00 99 98 97

To Lucy and Annie,
who gave us emotional support,
slept with us, licked us,
and waited patiently
to be taken to the park to pee

Disclaimer

We made every attempt here to exclude jokes that were attributed to comics, writers, and any known source. These jokes came from our mousepotato friends, who got them from their mousepotato friends, and we thank all them all. The jokes in this book are, as far as we can ascertain, the equivalent of the little moronic folktales people used to tell at cocktail parties or by the office watercooler. If anyone can prove authorship of any of these jokes, we will gladly attribute him in subsequent editions or leave the jokes out or kiss his ass or her ass (as the ass might be).

Who We Are

Alice Kahn is the author of three collections of humorous writing: *Multiple Sarcasm*, *My Life as a Gal*, and *Luncheon at the Café Ridiculous*, as well as the novel *Fun With Dirk and Bree*. She has been a syndicated columnist for the *Los Angeles Times Syndicate*, a staff writer for the *San Francisco Chronicle*, a nurse, a high school teacher, a poet, and a pauper. Her writing has appeared in magazines and newspapers ranging from *Playboy* to *Good Housekeeping*, *The New York Times* to the *Wall Street Journal*. She has appeared on numerous radio and television shows, including *Fresh Air*, *Prairie Home Companion*, and *The Charlie Rose Show*. She is currently a nurse-practitioner and a contributor to Microsoft Sidewalk.

John Dobby Boe is the author of a collection, *Life Itself: Messiness Is Next to Goddessness and Other Essays*. His writing has appeared in magazines and newspapers ranging from *California* to *The Utne Reader*, *The Chicago Reader* to *Psychological Perspectives*. He is Director of the Campus Writing Center at the University of California at Davis, where he teaches writing, edits the journal *Writing on the Edge*, and where he helped pioneer the computers and composition program. He is also a performance artist and storyteller who has been featured at festivals, conventions, on radio, and on television, including ABC's *20/20*. He has performed three one-man shows accompanied by the Steve Slagle Trio: *The Bongo Poet and Other Stories about Music*, *Erotic Folktales*, and *Italo Calvino's Italian Folktales*.

CONTENTS

Introduction: How People Really Use E-Mail

OLD JOKES, NEW JOKES, Jew jokes, blue jokes. They pop up on your computer screen, annoying intrusions into (or welcome transportation out of) your goddamn workplace. Usually the jokes are preceded by an endless list of sometimes distinguished names: Henry Kissinger <HKiss@Harvard.edu>, Bill Gates <Pearly@msn.con>, William Jefferson Clinton <SWillie@whitehouse.com>, Paula Jones <herass@trailertrash. net>, etc. These names reveal the checkered path of the joke. Sometimes scrolling through the names takes so long you give up and never get to the jokes.

> Q: *Don't these people have anything better to do?*
> A: *No.*

Sending dumb/dirty/politically incorrect (and occasionally actually funny) jokes by e-mail has become the most common form of high-tech social intercourse. E-mail joking has the advantage of looking like work (after all you're staring at your computer and moving your fingers) and feeling suspiciously like masturbation.

For the sender, it also has the advantage of contacting someone without having to say anything original. In an age of telecommunication, e-mail is the ultimate noncommunication. You'd call, but you might not get the answering machine.

> *Jewish mother: You never call, you never write, you never visit.*

Dutiful Son: Your joke is in the e-mail.

For the receivee, it's an ambiguous pleasure: finding a hundred new messages in the mailbox and discovering they're all bad jokes. Two of us are writing this: Alice, of the annoyed get-these-perverts-off-my-monitor state of mind, and Dobby, of the oh-goodie-new-e-mail state of mind. He opens his e-mail jokes as if they were presents (but as with presents, he is often disappointed).

Every single joke in this book was received by e-mail in a period of one year. Sometimes they arrived from senders we hadn't seen or spoken to in years. We marched together in the Sixties, lost touch having kids in the Seventies or making money in the Eighties, and then boom: "Did ya' hear the one about the pussy who couldn't purr?"

E-mail jokers will send you jokes they wouldn't have the nerve to say out loud. No matter how distinguished or politically correct the senders, they can't resist the shock value of sending the filthiest or most racist joke they have ever heard to twenty people at once. There, in a click of the mouse, it's done. On the other end, the joke arrives as an act of not-so-passive aggression—modem-assisted impulsive exhibitionism. The beauty of e-mail is it lets you make an obscene phone call and appear innocent at the same time. It's just a joke.

Q: I've got a huge hard drive that wants you to turn it on.
A: That's not funny!

How did e-mail evolve from a major tool of communication to a major form of goofing off and not communicating? It's a tribute to the indomitable human spirit that as the environment is destroyed and civilization crumbles, we have taken history's greatest technological tool and put it to *no good purpose*.

But you do get a few laughs.

We estimate the ratio of good jokes to bad that we've received via e-mail to be one to twenty. The jokes you are about to read have been carefully culled by professional humorists to reflect the cream of the crap. Reading these, you may not think we have standards. But every joke in here was scrupulously audited by two people off drugs. We have excluded 99.5 percent of blonde jokes, which take up an amazing amount of disk space and are said to be responsible for the detumescence of hard disks worldwide. We have also excluded all jokes that mentioned turds in chili.

> Q: *Why did you include that joke?*
>
> A: *It was my co-writer's decision.*

So what have we done for you, dear reader, lately? We have attempted to place the jokes we could stomach into major categories. We will explain our thinking briefly before each section, allowing the uninterested reader to skip our so-called thinking completely and go directly to the jokes. Our categories will, for example, allow the reader who loves jokes about what filthy scum men and women are to completely avoid ethnic jokes. We know you have your standards, so rather than totally suck up to common mores we have neatly arranged things in self-contained, fenced-in piles of jokes.

But we have four other caveats:

1. The Beluga Caveat: If the fu shits, don't read it.
2. If you don't get it: Hey, what's your problem?

3. There are d-u-m-b jokes here, but they are nowhere near as totally stupid as the ones we trashed.

4. The Humorist's Golden Rule: If any of these jokes offend you, kiss my ass.

Men Are from Uranus, Women Just Suck

THE WAR BETWEEN THE SEXES is out of control. Some say sexually transmitted diseases, birth control devices, women in the workplace, and daytime talk shows are the triggers for this escalation. Or maybe the problem is too much cybersex and not enough face time.

> Man: I'm sitting at my computer, and my disk is getting very, very hard
>
> Woman: I'm sitting in bed with my laptop popping.
>
> Man: I'm getting up and taking off my pants.
>
> Woman: I'm getting up and printing this.

Unlike the great themes in romantic literature, the themes of the jokes in the following section are crude and simple, namely:

> Q. Who are men?
>
> A. Humans with penises, who will say anything to get laid
>
> Q. Who are women?
>
> A. Humans with vaginas, who will put up with men, but could just as happily do it with a liverwurst.

In the last two decades we have been bombarded with helpful books teaching the correct ways to mate. The main result is that men and women seem to be hating each other more and more and gettin' less and less.

Feminism hasn't been entirely helpful. Some men accuse it of spreading the gospel that all a woman really needs is a sperm donor, sensible shoes, and a strap-on dildo. The antifeminist male reaction has contributed little more than inflatable dolls, the pole-dancing craze, and male bonding. Everybody's getting in touch with their feelings but getting felt up a lot less.

Some people say men and women must communicate better. For example:

> *Man: Wanna fuck?*
>
> *Woman: Let's dialogue that.*
>
> *Man: Wanna have sex?*
>
> *Woman: You still don't get it.*
>
> *Man: Wanna mess around?*
>
> *Woman: That's better, but still not good enough.*
>
> *Man: I love you. Wanna cuddle and let me kiss your ass?*
>
> *Woman: Okay.*

Maybe the problem is that too many people go to college these days, and academia, known to make anything boring, has even made sex boring. You can take a gender studies course and read such enlightening papers as "The Social Utility of Castration Anxiety," "Post-Modern Pheromones: Cigar Smoke as Turn-On," or "Buy Me Something: The Vagina's Hidden Text in Capitalist Culture."

Who wants to go out after that?

Psychobabbling women and sissy male psychologists tell us the problem is that women are feeling creatures and men are stupid assholes. But as one poor schmuck observed recently, "Hey, contempt and hatred are feelings too."

Forget academia, forget psychology, forget the war between men and women. Do something today for someone you love: Slip your sweetums a little joke.

>> SUBJECT: Men Are from Uranus, Women Just Suck

>> A guy is set up on a blind date. He goes to pick the woman up at her elegant high-rise apartment. He rings the bell and hears her call out, "Please come on in. I'm not quite ready yet. Make yourself at home, and I'll be with you in a moment."

So the man sits down in the living room. Suddenly, this yappy little dog comes into the room with a rubber ball in his mouth. The woman calls out from another room: "Oh, that's Skippy. He loves to play fetch. Feel free to play with him while I finish getting ready."

The dog is becoming very persistent about playing fetch, so the man gently tosses the ball to him. The dog goes running after it and comes right back. The man then tosses it a little harder this time. Again, the dog chases it and comes running right back.

So the man tosses the ball a little harder. It bounces twice, out onto the balcony and over the railing. The dog automatically goes chasing after it, jumps on a deck chair, and over the railing he goes, falling twelve stories to the pavement below. The man is horrified and goes to the railing to take a look.

Just then his date emerges, ready to go to dinner. She is absolutely stunning. The man is very nervous—it doesn't help that his date is also witty, warm, and affectionate. They have a marvelous time at dinner, getting along perfectly. The man has relaxed, until his date asks, "How did you like Skippy?"

This is the moment the man has been dreading. He takes a long sip of wine, and his expression is very serious. In a low and gentle voice, he replies, "Well, I'm no expert in this type of thing, but to me, he looked a little depressed."

>> A businessman boards a flight and is lucky enough to be seated next to an absolutely gorgeous woman. They exchange brief "hellos," and he notices she is reading a manual about sexual statistics.

He asks her about it, and she replies, "This is a very interesting book about sexual statistics. It says that American Indians, on average, have the longest penises and Polish men have the biggest average diameters. By the way, my name is Jill. What's yours?"

He cooly replies, "Tonto Kawalski. Nice to meet you."

>> If a man speaks in the forest and there is no woman around to hear him, is he still wrong?

>> A depressed young woman was so desperate that she decided to end her life by throwing herself into the ocean. When she went down to the docks, a handsome young sailor noticed her tears, took pity on her,

and said, "Look, you've got a lot to live for. I'm off to Europe in the morning, and if you like, I can stow you away on my ship. I'll take good care of you and bring you food every day."

Moving closer, he slipped his arm around her shoulder and added, "I'll keep you happy, and you'll keep me happy."

The girl nodded yes. After all, what did she have to lose? That night, the sailor brought her aboard and hid her in a lifeboat. From then on, every night he brought her three sandwiches and a piece of fruit, and they made passionate love until dawn.

Three weeks later, during a routine inspection, she was discovered by the captain. "What are you doing here?" the captain asked.

"I have an arrangement with one of the sailors," she explained. "He's taking me to Europe, and he's screwing me."

"He sure is, lady," said the captain. "This is the Staten Island ferry."

>> Four Pickup Lines

I like every muscle in your body, especially mine.

The word is "legs." Why don't we go to my place and spread the word?

Wanna come up and see my EtchASketch?

I'm taking an educational survey: How do you like to do it?

>> Q: Why do women have breasts?

A: So men will talk to them.

>> Q: What's the useless flesh attached to a penis called?

A: A man.

>> Q: What do you call a woman with no asshole?

A: Divorced.

>> Q: Why does it take five women with PMS to change a lightbulb?

A: Because it just fucking does all right!

>> Q: How do you make a woman scream after an orgasm?

A: Wipe your dick on the curtains.

>> A butcher who lived over his shop was awakened one night by strange noises from below. He tiptoed downstairs and observed his twenty-year-old daughter sitting on the chopping block, stimulating herself with a liverwurst.

With a heavy sigh, he tiptoed back to bed. The next morning, a customer came in the shop and asked for liverwurst. "I don't have any," replied the butcher.

Annoyed, the customer pointed at the used liverwurst and said, "No liverwurst, eh? So what's that hanging on a hook right over there?"

The butcher frowned and replied, "That, madam, is my goddamn son-in-law."

>> One day, after a near eternity in the Garden of Eden, Adam calls out to God, "Lord, I have a problem."

"What's the problem, Adam?" God asks.

"Lord, you created me and provided for me and surrounded me with this beautiful garden and all of these wonderful animals, but I'm just not happy."

"Why is that, Adam?" comes the reply from the heavens.

"Lord, I know you created this place for me, with all this lovely food and all of the beautiful animals, but I am lonely."

"Well Adam, in that case I have the perfect solution. I shall create a woman for you."

"What's a woman, Lord?"

"This woman will be the most intelligent, sensitive, caring, and beautiful creature I have ever created. She will be so intelligent that she can figure out what you want before you want it. She will be so sensitive and caring that she will know your every mood and how to make you happy. Her beauty will rival that of the heavens and earth. She will unquestioningly care for your every need and desire. She will be the perfect companion for you," replies the heavenly voice. "She will love you before her self."

"Sounds great!"

"She will be, but this is going to cost you, Adam."

"How much will this woman cost me, Lord?" Adam replies.

"She'll cost you your right arm, your right leg, an eye, an ear, and your left testicle."

Adam ponders this for some time, with a look of deep thought and concern. Finally Adam says to God, "What can I get for a rib?"

>> Mother is in the kitchen making supper for her family when her youngest daughter walks in.

Child: Mother, where do babies come from?

Mom: Well dear, a mommy and a daddy fall in love and get married. One night they go into their room and they kiss and hug and have sex. [The daughter looks puzzled.] That means the daddy puts his penis in the mommy's vagina. That's how you get a baby, honey.

Child: Oh, I see, but the other night when I came into you and daddy's room, you had daddy's penis in your mouth. What do you get when you do that?

Mom: Jewelry, dear.

>> Q: Why do women have trouble achieving orgasm?

A: Who cares?

>> Q: Why do women have legs?

A: So they don't leave trails like little snails.

>> Q: What is the irritating part around a woman's vagina?

A: The woman

>> Q: Why should you never trust a women?

A: Well, would you trust anything that bled for three days and wouldn't die?

>> In 1890, a stagecoach bounced down a rutted road, heading for Dallas. In the coach were a Texan, a busty lady, and a greenhorn from the East. The green-horn kept eyeing the lady. Finally he leaned forward and said, "Lady, I'll give you ten dollars for a blow job." The Texan looked appalled, pulled out his pistol, and shot the greenhorn between the eyes.

The lady gasped and said, "Thank you, sir, for defending my honor."

The Texan holstered his gun and said, "Your honor, hell! Just trying to keep down inflation. Around here, a blow job goes for two dollars."

>> Seems God was just about done creating the universe and had a couple of leftover things in his bag of creations, so he stopped by to visit Adam and Eve in the Garden.

He told the couple that one of the things he had to give away was the ability to stand up and pee. "It's a very handy thing," God told the couple, who he found hanging around under an apple tree. "I was wondering if either one of you wanted that ability."

Adam flipped out, jumping up and begging, "Oh, give that to me! I'd love to be able to do that! It's just the sort of thing a man should do. Oh please, oh please, oh please, let me have that ability. It'd be so great! When I'm working in the garden or naming the animals, I could just let it rip. It'd be so cool. Oh please, God, let it be me who you give that gift to, let me stand and pee, oh please. . . ." On and on he went, like an excited little boy who had to pee.

Eve smiled and shook her head at the display. She told God that if Adam wanted it so badly—and it sure seemed to be the sort of thing that would make him happy—she really wouldn't mind if Adam were the one given the ability to stand up and pee.

And so it was. And it was . . . well, good.

"Fine," God said, looking back into his bag of left-over gifts. "Let's see what's left here? Oh yes, multiple orgasms. . ."

» A drunken blonde goes into a bar. The bartender asks her what she would like, and she replies, "Gimme a beer."

The bartender then asks, "Anheuser-Busch?"

To which she replies, "Fine thanks, and how's your cock?"

» An eighty-year-old woman came home one day and heard strange noises in her bedroom. She opened the door and discovered her forty-year-old daughter playing with her vibrator.

"What are you doing?" asked the mom.

"Mom, I am forty years old, and look at me. I am ugly. I will never get married, so this is pretty much my husband." The mother walked out of the room shaking her head.

The next day the father entered the room and found his daughter using the vibrator. "What the hell are you doing?" he asked.

His daughter replied, "I already told Mom. I'm forty years old now and ugly. I will never get married, so this is as close as I'll ever get to a husband." The father walked out of the room shaking his head too.

The next day, the mother came home to find her husband with a beer in one hand and the vibrator in the other, watching the football game. "For Chrissakes! What are you doing?" she cried.

The husband replied, "What does it look like I'm doing? I'm having a beer and watching the game with my new son-in-law!"

>> Little Johnny comes home with a homework paper to do. He asks his dad to help him write about the difference between theory and reality.

His dad says, "Go to your mom and ask her if she would sleep with another man for a million dollars." Little Johnny does as he is told, and Mom says, "Well, yes, I suppose I would."

His dad then says, "Now go ask your big sister if she would sleep with another man for a million dollars." Little Johnny does this too, and Sis says, "Yes, I suppose I would."

Little Johnny and his dad then sit down, and Dad says, "Now son, you've learned the difference between theory and reality. In theory, we're sitting on two million dollars. In reality, we're living with a couple of whores."

>> This guy is stranded on a desert island with Cindy Crawford. He's cool, and he doesn't make any moves toward her for several weeks. Finally, one day, he asks her if maybe they could start up a physical relationship, to attend to each other's needs. Cindy says she is game, and a very nice sexual relationship begins.

Everything is great for about four months. One day the guy goes to Cindy and says, "I'm having this problem. It's kind of a guy thing, but I need to ask you a favor." Cindy says, "Okay."

The guy says "Can I borrow your eyebrow pencil?" and Cindy looks at him a little funny, but says, "Sure, you can borrow my eyebrow pencil."

The guy then says, "Do you mind if I use the eyebrow pencil to draw a mustache on you?" Cindy is getting a little worried but says, "Okay."

Then the guy says, "Can you wear some of my guy clothing? I need for you to look more like a man." Cindy is getting a little disappointed at this point but says, "Well, I guess so."

Then the guy says to Cindy, "Do you mind if I call you Fred?" Cindy, very dejected, says, "I guess not."

So the guy reaches out and grabs Cindy by the arms and says, "Fred, you won't believe who I've been sleeping with these past four months!"

The Computer Is God; Bill Gates Is Great (Satan)

SHOULDN'T THE BEST JOKES being passed around electronically be about computers? But *reductio ad abnerdum*: no such luck. Geeks say the darndest things, but they just aren't that funny.

OK, you've got your hard-disk jokes, your software jokes, your byte-me jokes—not the worst of the lot. In fact, if we eliminated all the bad computer jokes, this section would be empty, and we decided you can't have a book about e-mail jokes without including the Best of the Computer Jokes Which Tend Toward the Lame Anyway.

> Q: *Did you hear about the guy who invented a laptop that comes with an internal vibrator?*
>
> A: *He calls it a laptop dancer.*

Half of the computer jokes sent to us by e-mail feature Bill Gates at the pearly gates, which only proves that a lot of people spend a lot of time sitting at their computers wishing Bill Gates were dead. Of course, we're all jealous of the money he's made, but there are better reasons to hate him:

1. Windows 95.

2. Office 97.

3. Serial Killer Apps.

4. Turned Apple into Beta.

5. He is the devil.

The problem with computer jokes is that they tend to be in-industry jokes that rely on jargon, the latest industry gossip, and not having a life. If you don't do Windows, you miss half the jokes. If you do do Windows, you're so deep in the do-do that the jokes aren't funny.

Computer humor has failed to notice some of the things that are funny about the industry, like instant obsolescence. If we were computers, we would have been upgraded fourteen times by now. We'd have a better memory and more RAM, and we'd take up less space. We'd also be incompatible with most other humans. In short, we'd be a lot like the Great Satan himself—Gates.

There are many diabolical things about Microsoft products. For example, if you're using Word and try to type the computer indicator for a joke, the famed "smiley" composed of a : and a), Word will automatically turn the parenthesis into a ☺. I don't want a fucking ☺, but the auto-Nazi won't stop. I want to kill the ☺. Die ☺ ! Have a shitty day!

There are also forced grammatical oppressions on Word, such as the instant-correction that makes you capitalize Internet. Like it's bill gates himself, or god for that matter—neither of which self-capitalize. Which either proves that the internet really is god or that you'd better learn to love squiggly red lines.

Perhaps the Unabomber was on the right track when he thought that computers were evil. But unfortunately, with his bizarre, random choice of victims, he was the ultimate Polish joke.

> Q: Hey, Kaczynski, what are you going to do about the fact that computers are taking over the world?

A: I'm killing everyone with "tree" in his name.

We keep hearing about how computers will take over our lives, will raise our children, keep track of our money, and turn on our sprinklers. But as long as e-mail jokes are the main contribution of this new medium, we're safe.

>> SUBJECT: Computers Are God; Bill Gates Is Great (Satan)

>> Three women were sitting around talking about their husbands' performances as lovers. The first woman says "My husband works as a marriage counselor. He always buys me flowers and candy before we make love. I like that."

The second woman says, "My husband is a motorcycle mechanic. He likes to play rough and slaps me around sometimes. I kinda like that."

The third woman just shakes her head and says, "My husband works for Microsoft. He just sits on the edge of the bed and tells me how great it's going to be when I get it."

>> Bill Gates, Andy Grove, and Steve Jobs are in a high-powered business meeting. During the serious, tense discussion, a beeping noise suddenly comes from where Bill is sitting. Bill says, "Oh, that's my beeper. Gentlemen, excuse me, I need to take this call." So Bill lifts his wristwatch to his ear and

begins talking into the end of his tie. After completing the call, he notices the others are staring at him. Bill explains, "Oh, this is my new emergency communication system. I have an earpiece built into my watch and a microphone sewn into the end of my tie. That way I can take a call anywhere." The others nod, and the meeting continues.

Five minutes later, the discussion is again interrupted when Andy starts beeping. He says, "Excuse me, gentlemen, this must be an important call." So Andy taps his earlobe and begins talking into thin air. When he completes his call, he notices the others staring at him and explains, "I also have an emergency communication system. But my earpiece is actually implanted in my earlobe, and the microphone is actually embedded in this fake tooth." The others nod, and the meeting continues.

Five minutes later, the discussion is again interrupted when Steve emits a thunderous fart. He looks up at the others staring at him and says, "Somebody get me a piece of paper. I'm receiving a fax."

>> Geek pickup line: Hey, baby, if I point will you click?

>> A member of the Windows 95 programming team dies. On his arrival at the pearly gates, St. Peter tells him that he can choose where he would like to spend eternity: heaven or hell.

The programmer says, "Great, but is it possible to take a quick peek at both places first, so I can make up my mind?"

"No problemo!" says St. Peter, so they head down to see hell.

Strangely enough, hell seems to be a great place: lots of beer, good music, pretty girls, and people having a good time—kind of like an eternal beach party!

The programmer is amazed. "If this is hell, I'm really looking forward to seeing heaven!" So they take the elevator up to heaven and take a look there. Heaven is quite different: a bunch of people dressed in white robes, sporting wigs and haloes and sitting around on clouds playing harps, pleasant enough, but a bit dull.

Thinking it over quickly, the programmer tells St. Peter that he wants to go to hell. "OK," says St. Peter, who snaps his fingers and off to hell the programmer goes.

To the programmer's consternation, hell turns out to be quite a different place than he was led to believe: fire, brimstone, the sounds of people wailing and gnashing their teeth—in short, suffering without relief! The programmer is deeply disappointed, and demands an audience with Satan himself so he can lodge a complaint. "What's the problem?" asks Satan.

"Well, I chose to go to hell because it looked like a great place, but when I got here it was nothing like what I saw!"

"Ah," says the Devil as an evil grin spreads over his countenance, "I guess you only saw the demo."

>> Reaching the end of a job interview, the human resources person asked the young computer engineer

fresh out of college, "And what starting salary were you looking for?"

The computer engineer said, "In the neighborhood of $100,000 a year, depending on the benefits package."

The HR person said, "Well, what would you say to a package of six-weeks' vacation, fourteen paid holidays, full medical and dental, a company matching retirement fund to 50 percent of salary, and a company car leased every two years—say, a red Corvette?"

The computer engineer sat up straight and said, "Wow! Are you kidding?"

And the HR person said, "Certainly, but you started it."

>> FAQs

Q: How many Microsoft vice presidents does it take to change a lightbulb?

A: Five. One to work the bulb and four to make sure that Microsoft gets two dollars for every lightbulb ever changed anywhere in the world.

Q: How many Microsoft tech-support people does it take to change a lightbulb?

A: Please continue to hold. Your call is very important to us.

Q: How many Microsoft technicians does it take to change a lightbulb?

A: Three. Two to hold the ladder and one to hammer the bulb into a faucet.

Q: How many Microsoft testers does it take to change a lightbulb?

A: We just determine that the room is dark; we don't actually change the bulb. Since we have a dead-bulb result on file from a previous test, rest assured that development is working on a bug fix.

Q: How many Microsoft shipping department personnel does it take to change a lightbulb?

A: We can change the bulb in seven to ten working days. If you call before 2 PM and pay an extra fifteen dollars, we can get the bulb changed overnight. Don't forget to put your name in the upper right-hand corner of the lightbulb box.

Q: How many Windows users does it take to change a lightbulb?

A: Five. But they'll swear up and down that it was *just* as easy as it would be for a Mac user.

Q: How many Microsoft managers does it take to change a lightbulb?

A: We've formed a task force to study the problem.

Q: How many Microsoft engineers does it take to change a lightbulb?

A: None. Bill Gates will just redefine Darkness™ as the new industry standard.

>> Three engineers are riding in a car: an electrical engineer, a chemical engineer, and a Microsoft engineer. Suddenly the car stalls and stops by the side

of the road. The three engineers look at each other with bewilderment, wondering what could be wrong.

The electrical engineer, not knowing much about mechanics, suggests, "Let's strip down the electronics of the car and try to trace where a fault might have occurred."

The chemical engineer, not knowing much about electronics, suggests, "Maybe the fuel has become emulsified and is causing a blockage somewhere in the system."

The Microsoft engineer suggests, "Why don't we close all the windows, get out, get back in, open the windows again, and maybe it will work."

» Hear about the woman who married three different Microsoft employees and still died a virgin?

Her first husband was in Training, and he kept teaching her how to do it herself. The second one was in Sales, and he kept telling her how good it was going to be in the next release. The third was in Tech Support, and he kept saying, "Don't worry, it'll be up any minute now. . . ."

World
Wide
Wed

OH THE HORROR, the unspeakable horror of being chained to another so-called human being for the rest of time. How sweet death can look under such circumstances.

Perhaps that's why blood, murder, and violence pop up so frequently in good marriage jokes. The bliss of marriage has led more than one poor soul to the Bruno Magli shoe store.

There are many wonderful things to treasure in a long-term marriage. Here are a few:

1. Never having to say "I love you."
2. Someone else to hate the kids.
3. You can fart in bed.
4. Not speaking doesn't mean you're fighting.
5. You can do it with your eyes closed and one hand tied behind your back.
6. Someone to sell down the river when you're indicted in Whitewater.
7. Legal pickpocketing.
8. The Zen of boredom; the hell of companionship.
9. Your whole life was foreplay.
10. Division of Labor: You work like a dog; I'll sit here and lick my genitals.

We joke about marriage as we would any other painful subject. We, of course, are two happily married people. Not to each other. How else could we slave over these jokes and not use them as weapons against each other? We granted each other immunity.

Dobby would not spare his own wife, Judy. When Judy came home after her recent mammogram, she was annoyed at his lack of sympathy for having had her breasts put through the ringer. "How would you like to have your balls in a vise?" she asked Dobby. "Thank you, but I'm already married," he replied.

Alice's husband, when asked to explain the secret of his thirty-year enchantment with the lovely Alice, said "Lack of imagination."

Seriously, there really is a wonderful side to this yoking business. At least now you can commit adultery. While we know nothing of this dark side of marriage, we are aware that without marriage, there would be no adultery jokes.

> Q: *Why did the moron marry Lady Moron?*
>
> A: *To get more on the side.*

Actually adultery is not "adult," as in an adult movie or an adult bookstore or an adult community (where old people do dirty things). It turns out that the word actually relates to "spoiling" (ruining), as in "unadulterated bullshit." No doubt about it, real adultery can make a marriage go sour. But the adultery fantasy, as any one-hundred-buck-an-hour marriage counselor or lap dancer will tell you, is good for you. Go with it!

That's what these jokes actually do. There are two dominant themes in marriage jokes (and one dominatrix in each marriage): adultery, which relieves your misery, and death, which finally ends it.

Certainly we don't mean to sound negative about marriage here. We dedicate this section of jokes filled with pain and misery and longing to our beloved spouses, Judy and Eddie, till death or swinging in the old-age home do us part.

>> SUBJECT: World Wide Wed

>> Have you heard about the three stages of sex in marriage? First, when you're newlyweds, there's all-over-the-house-sex. This is when you just do it wherever the mood strikes.

Second, is bedroom sex. This is when you've been married long enough that the only place you want to have sex is in the bedroom.

Third, after many years, you are left with hallway sex. This is when you pass each other in the hallway and say "Screw you" and "Screw you, too!"

>> A husband and wife were going to a costume party. He was dressed as a bull and she was a heifer. On the way to the party, their car ran out of gas. As they were walking to the gas station, they decided to take a shortcut through a field. All of a sudden a bull came charging up. "Oh no," cried the wife. "What are we going to do?"

"Well, honey," replied the husband, "I'm going to bend over and act like I'm grazing. I suggest you brace yourself."

>>A cannibal and his son are hiding behind some bushes, waiting for some food to stroll by.

After a few minutes, a skinny guy comes along. The son says, "How about him, Dad?"

"Naw," says the father. "Too skinny."

A while later a fat guy wanders by. "What about that guy, Dad?" asks the son.

"Naw. Too much cholesterol."

A little later, a foxy chick wriggles by. The son asks, "How about her, Dad?"

"Absolutely. Let's take her home and eat your mother!"

>> Mickey Mouse decided he wanted to get a divorce, so he went to a judge and told him his problems. The judge listened and then said, "Mickey, I don't know if I can give you this divorce. You are a national symbol. Everyone knows you. Kids look up to you. You can't divorce Minnie just because she is a little silly."

Mickey said, "I didn't say she was a little silly. I said she was fucking Goofy."

>> A couple have been married forty years and are revisiting the same places they went to on their honeymoon. As they are driving through the secluded countryside, they pass a ranch with a tall deer fence running along the road.

The woman says, "Sweetheart, let's do the same thing we did here forty years ago."

The guy stops the car. His wife backs against the fence, and he immediately jumps her like a bass on a june bug. They make love like never before.

Back in the car, the guy says, "Darlin', you sure never moved like that forty years ago—or any time since that I can remember."

The woman says, "Forty years ago that goddamn fence wasn't electrified!"

» A married couple was enjoying a dinner out when a statuesque blonde walked over to their table, exchanged warm greetings with the husband, and walked off.

"Who was that?" the wife demanded.

"If you must know," the husband replied, "that was my mistress."

"Your mistress? That's it! I want a divorce!" the wife fumed.

The husband looked her straight in the eye and said, "So you want to risk giving up our big house in the suburbs, your Mercedes, your furs, your jewelry, and our vacation home in Mexico?"

For a long time they continued dining in silence.

Finally, the woman nudged her husband and said, "Isn't that Howard over there? Who's he with?"

"That's *his* mistress," her husband replied.

"Oh," she said, taking a bite of dessert. "Ours is much cuter."

>> A husband and wife are driving when they get pulled over by a policeman. The policeman goes up to the car and asks for the man's license.

The man replies, "Why do you need my license? What did I do wrong?"

The policeman answers, "You were traveling forty-five miles per hour in a thirty-miles-per-hour zone."

"Come on, officer," the man replies, "you know I was only going thirty-five."

"No, you weren't!" interrupts the wife. "I told you you were speeding. I told you not to go fast. I knew you'd get a ticket."

"Shut up." grunts the husband.

The policeman continues, "I'm also charging you for going through a red light."

"Officer," the man explains, "you know as well as I, that light was yellow, not red."

The wife pipes in, "No, it was most definitely red. I told you it was red. I told you."

At this point the husband is infuriated. He yells at his wife, "Shut up!"

The policeman exclaims, "Hey! Stop yelling at your wife!" He then turns to the wife and asks, "Does he always talk to you this way?"

She calmly replies, "No, only when he's been drinking."

>> "Children, I'd like you to close your eyes and taste these," announced the teacher. Without difficulty, they managed to identify the tastes of cherries,

lemons, and mint, but when the teacher had them put honey-flavored Lifesavers in their mouths, every one of the children was stumped.

"I'll give you a hint," said the teacher. "It's something your daddy and mommy probably call each other all the time."

Instantly, one of the children spat the Lifesaver out of his mouth and shouted, "Spit 'em out, you guys, they're assholes!"

>> Bill worked in a pickle factory. He had been employed there for a number of years when he came home one day to confess to his wife that he had a terrible compulsion. He had an urge to stick his penis into the pickle slicer. His wife suggested that he should see a sex therapist to talk about it, but Bill indicated that he'd be too embarrassed. He vowed to overcome the compulsion on his own.

One day a few weeks later, Bill came home absolutely ashen. His wife could see at once that something was seriously wrong. "What's wrong, Bill?" she asked.

"Do you remember that I told you how I had this tremendous urge to put my penis into the pickle slicer?"

"Oh, Bill, you didn't."

"Yes, I did."

"My God, Bill, what happened?"

"I got fired."

"No, Bill. I mean, what happened with the pickle slicer?"

"Oh . . . she got fired too."

>> A man placed some flowers on the grave of his departed mother and started back for his car, which was parked on the cemetery road. His attention was diverted to a man kneeling at a grave. The man seemed to be praying with profound intensity and kept repeating, "Why did you die? Why did you die?"

The first man approached him and said, "Sir, I don't want to interfere with your private grief, but this demonstration of hurt and pain is more than I've ever seen before. For whom do you mourn so deeply? Your child? A parent? Who, may I ask, lies in that grave?"

The mourner answered, "My wife's first husband. Why did you die? Why did you die?"

>> "Dear," said the wife. "What would you do if I died?"

"Why, dear, I would be extremely upset," said the husband. "Why do you ask such a question?"

"Would you remarry?" persevered the wife.

"No, of course not, dear," said the husband.

"Don't you like being married?" said the wife.

"Of course I do, dear," he said.

"Then why wouldn't you remarry?"

"All right," said the husband, "I'd remarry."

"You would?" said the wife, looking vaguely hurt.

"Yes," said the husband.

"Would you sleep with her in our bed?" said the wife after a long pause.

"Well yes, I suppose I would," replied the husband.

"I see," said the wife indignantly. "And would you let her wear my old clothes?"

"I suppose, if she wanted to," said the husband.

"Really," said the wife icily. "And would you take down the pictures of me and replace them with pictures of her?"

"Yes. I think that would be the correct thing to do."

"Is that so?" said the wife, leaping to her feet. "And I suppose you'd let her play with my golf clubs, too."

"Of course not, dear," said the husband. "She's left-handed."

>> These three guys, separately, go for interviews with the CIA.

The first guy has his interview, and at the end the interviewer says, "OK, I really like you, and I'm prepared to offer you a job. The final test you have is the loyalty test. We have your wife in the back room; take this gun, go in there, and kill her."

The guy goes in, but comes out again five minutes later and says, "Here, take the gun back. I couldn't do it. I love my wife. I guess I'm just not cut out for the CIA."

The second guy goes in for his interview. Same thing: "Here's a gun. Go in, and kill your wife."

Again, the guy comes out five minutes later and admits that he couldn't do it.

The third guy also has a successful interview. He disappears into the back room with the gun, and immediately the interviewer hears three gunshots, followed swiftly by crashing and wrecking noises. Two minutes later the guy comes out again, tie crooked, hair disheveled, panting and sweating. "Congratulations," says the interviewer. "You start on Monday. But tell me, what was all the noise about? You look a mess."

And the guy replies, "Some idiot put blanks in the gun, so I had to beat her to death with a chair."

>> After a quarrel, a wife said to her husband, "You know, I was a fool when I married you."

And the husband replied, "Yes, dear, but I was in love and didn't notice it."

>> A woman was telling her friend, "It is I who made my husband a millionaire."

"And what was he before you married him?" asked the friend.

The woman replied, "A multimillionaire."

>> A young couple is sitting at the kitchen table one night discussing their dismal finances. The only solution they can come up with is for the wife to go out at night and turn a few tricks. So the next night she gets all dolled up and they drive to "that part of town." The husband parks across the street

from where the wife will be plying her trade. After the wife stands on the corner for a few minutes, a car pulls up, and the man inside asks her, "How much for the whole works?"

The woman runs across the street and asks her husband how much to charge. The husband says, "Tell him one hundred dollars for the works."

The woman runs back to the john and tells him the price. The man says that's too much and asks the woman, "How much for a hand job?"

The woman runs back across the street to consult with her husband who tells her to charge forty dollars for a hand job. The woman runs back to the john, who agrees on the price. He proceeds to pull down his pants and the wife is surprised to see the man's twelve-inch penis.

At this point she runs one last time to her husband across the street and says, "Honey, can you lend me sixty dollars?"

>> A sixty-five-year-old woman is in the bedroom jumping up and down on the bed, singing and laughing like a child. In comes her husband, watches for a moment, and asks, "Woman, what's come over you? You look ridiculous."

She says, "I've just been to the doctor for my physical exam, and he told me I have the breasts of an eighteen year old," and resumes jumping.

"Yeah, sure," harrumphs the old man, "But what did he say about your sixty-five-year-old ass?"

The woman responds, "Actually, your name never came up."

>> A man meets his old-time friend for the customary holiday drinks, and after exchanging pleasantries, they inquire about each other and their families.

He says to his friend, "Well, things are OK, but I'm really concerned about my wife's health lately."

The friend asks, "Goodness, what seems to be the matter. Last time I saw her she looked the picture of health."

The man says, "That's what's so puzzling; we went to the doctors, and they just can't diagnose the problem with her. They say it could be one of two things: Either she's got AIDS or she's got Alzheimer's. I'm so worried I don't know what to do!"

His friend says, "Let me give you some advice. If I were you I'd take her for a long drive out of town, park, take a walk, and then leave her and drive away. If she finds her way back home, I wouldn't fuck her."

>> Doris and Fred, having started their retirement years, decide to raise some extra cash by advertising for a lodger in their house. After a few days, a young attractive woman applies for the room and explains that she is a model working in a nearby Manchester studio for a few weeks and that she would like the room for Mondays to Thursdays but would pay for the whole week. Doris shows her the house and they agree to start straightaway. "There's just one problem," explains the model. "Because of my job I have to have a bath every night, and I notice you don't have a bath."

"That's not a problem," replies Doris. "We have a tin bathtub out in the yard, and we bring it into the living room, set it in front of the fire, and fill it with hot water."

"What about your husband?" asks the model.

"Oh, he plays darts most weekdays, so he will be out in the evenings," replies Doris.

"Good," says the model. "That being settled, I'll go to the studio and see you tonight."

That evening Fred dutifully goes to his darts match while Doris prepares the bath for the model. After stripping, the model steps into the bath, and Doris is amazed to see that she has no pubic hair. The model notices Doris's staring eyes, smiles, and explains that it is part of her job to shave her pussy, especially when modeling swimwear or under-clothes.

Later, when Fred returns, Doris relates this oddity, but he does not believe her. "It's true, I tell you," says Doris. "Look, if you don't believe me, tomorrow night I'll leave the curtains slightly open, and you can peek in and see for yourself."

The next night Fred leaves as usual, and Doris pre-pares the bath for the model. As the model steps naked into the bath, Doris, standing behind her, looks towards the curtains and points towards the model's naked pussy. Then she lifts up her skirt and, wearing no panties, points to her own hairy mass.

Later Fred returns and they retire to bed. "Well, do you believe me now?" she asks Fred.

"Yes," he replies. "I've never seen anything like it in my life. But why did you lift up your skirt and show your hairy twat?"

"Just to show you the difference," answers Doris. "But anyway you've seen my pussy millions of times."

"Yes," says Fred, "I have. But the rest of the fucking darts team hasn't!"

>> Q: What's the difference between your wife and your job?

A: After ten years the job still sucks.

>> Now that they've retired, an old couple was discussing all aspects of their future. "What will you do if I die before you do?" he asked her.

After some thought, she said that she'd probably look for a house-sharing situation with three other single or widowed women who might be a little younger than herself, since she is so active for her age.

Then she asked him, "What will you do if I die first?"

He replied, "Probably the same thing."

>> It seems when Armstrong walked on the moon, he not only gave his famous "One Step for Man . . ." statement, but followed it by several remarks. It ended with "Good luck, Mr. Gorsky." Over the years many people have questioned him as to what the "Mr. Gorsky" statement meant. Two weeks ago, while answering questions following a speech, he finally responded.

It seems Mr. Gorsky had finally died, and so Armstrong felt he could answer.

When Armstrong was a kid, he was playing ball. His brother hit a fly which landed in front of the Gorsky's bedroom window. As he leaned down to pick it up, he heard Mrs. Gorsky shouting at Mr. Gorsky. "Oral sex! Oral sex you want? You'll get oral sex when the kid next door walks on the moon!"

4

Topical Humor: The Little Silly History of Our Times

FORGET LENO. Who needs Letterman? The morning paper is way too slow. In this fast, wow, now, come-on-a-dime world, is there any more important use for computers than topical jokes? We think not.

We include these of-the-moment jokes here knowing full well that they will seem dated by tomorrow, let alone by publication date.

> *Did you hear the one about Lincoln in the Clinton bedroom?*
>
> *"Four scores and seven inches ago . . . "*

See, that joke was funny when it went out on the Internet in 1865, but it seems dated now.

We all know that as soon as there's a disaster, mass murder, or famous pervert, all we have to do is sit at our screens and wait for the jokes to pop up.

A lot of these jokes aren't funny, and have a short half-life to them. But they form a kind of Little Silly History of Our Times.

Some of the recent stars of e-mail humor include O.J. Simpson, Lorena Bobbitt, Bob Packwood, the Unabomber, Michael Jackson, and the Clintons. By and large, they are people prominent for their peccadilloes or, in the case of Lorena Bobbitt, her peccadillectomy.

The ease with which people can create e-mail lists and send off favorite jokes was demonstrated in the notorious Vonnegut

MIT-speech incident. Although not a joke, the speech, written by a Chicago newspaper columnist but falsely attributed to Vonnegut, charmed people who immediately e-mailed it off to thousands. Like a message in the old game of telephone, it went around the world. It was the credibility of Vonnegut's name that led to the circle jerk sends. So from this day forth we will pepper our jokes with Kurt Vonnegut references.

> *If Vanna White married Kurt Vonnegut, she'd be Vanna Vonnegut.*

> *Q: What did Dr. Seuss call his book about Kurt Vonnegut living in Mongolia?*
> *A: The Kurt in the Yurt.*

> *Q: What is the distinguishing mark Paula Jones says is on President Clinton's penis?*
> *A: A profile of Kurt Vonnegut.*

OK, these may not seem funny now, but back in 1997. . . .

>> SUBJECT: Topical Humor (The Little Silly History of Our Times)

>> Bill Clinton observed a sign, "Screw Clinton," written in urine on the White House lawn. After an investigation, an FBI man told him that he had bad news.

"What's the bad news?"

"It's Al Gore's urine."

"Oh my God, my own vice president!"

"I'm afraid there's worse news, sir. It's Hillary's handwriting!"

>> Pat Buchanan dies and goes to hell. As he approaches the gates, the Devil is there to greet him. The Devil says, "Welcome to hell, Pat. I think you're really gonna like it here. Say Pat, while you were alive, were you much of a smoker?"

Buchanan replies, "Why yes, I was."

The Devil says, "Well in that case, you're going to *love* Fridays. On Fridays we get all the smokes we can handle, and we sit around and smoke, smoke, smoke, smoke until we can't smoke any more. And Pat, when you were alive, were you much of a drinker?"

Buchanan says, "Yes, as a matter of fact, I did drink from time to time."

The Devil smiles and says, "In that case, you're going to *love* Saturdays because on Saturday, we get free liquor, and we just drink and drink and drink and drink and drink. Oh, and Pat, when you were alive, were you a homosexual?"

Buchanan says, "No I was not!"

The Devil says, "Gee, in that case, you are going to *hate* Sundays!"

>> Q: What's the difference between O.J. and Simba?

A: Simba is an African Lion. . . .

>> Q: What did Bob Packwood say about the cute female campaign volunteer?

A: I want her on my staff

>> Former Vice-President Quayle, Speaker of the House Gingrich, and President Clinton are traveling in a car together in Kansas. A tornado comes along and whirls them up into the air and tosses them thousands of yards away. They all fall into a daze.

When they come to and extract themselves from the vehicle, they realize they're in the fabled land of Oz. They decide to go see the famous Wizard of Oz. The Wizard is known for granting people their wishes.

Quayle says, "I'm going to ask the Wizard for a brain."

Gingrich responds, "I'm going to ask the Wizard for a heart."

Clinton speaks up, "Where's Dorothy?"

>> With yet another young man in her life, Elizabeth Taylor decides that in her advancing years she needs to tighten up her vaginal area. She puts her trust in her plastic surgeon of thirty years standing, the one who had carried out her face-lifts, boob jobs, and ass-lifts. Sworn to secrecy, he agrees that only he would ever know about the operation. He carries out the delicate operation, carefully slicing away strips of the loose folds of skin. It is a long operation.

Liz awakens the next morning to see three "Get Well Soon" cards on her bedside table. She is appalled and demands to see the doctor. "No one but you should know about this! You have let me down," she says.

"Ah," says the doc, "this card is from my wife and me, wishing you a speedy recovery."

"How nice," says Liz. "Thank you. What a nice thought."

"The second card is from old Madge, the cleaner who has cleaned up after all your previous operations. She is to be trusted."

"What a beautiful thought from such a humble person. I'm really touched," she says. "But who is the third card from?" asks Liz.

"Oh," says the doctor, "that's from Evander Holyfield, thanking you for his new ear."

>> President Clinton flies into Andrews AFB. The color guard is present, as well as the commanding general. The general is standing at attention while President Clinton is descending the stairs. He notices that President Clinton has a pig tucked under his arm.

The general, not knowing quite what to say, simply blurts out, "Nice pig, sir."

President Clinton responds by saying, "You bet it is. It is a hand-fed, corn-fed, purebred razorback from Arkansas. I got it for Hillary.

Again the general is a bit tongue-tied, but without flinching he responds, "Nice trade, sir."

>> Michael Jackson went to the hospital to visit his wife and son. He found the doctor and asked him, "When can we have sex?"

The doctor answered, "Well, you better wait until he is about thirteen or so."

>> Q: What did Ellen DeGeneres say to Kathie Lee?

A: Can I be Frank with you?

>> Did you hear that Lorena Bobbitt got in an accident?

Yeah, some dick cut her off on the freeway.

>> Did you hear the news about Hitler? There's good news and there's bad. First the good news: They found Hitler. He's alive, living in Buenos Aires, and they're bringing him to trial. The bad news: They're holding the trial in L.A.

>> A beautiful but aging woman goes into a bar filled with photos of famous boxers. A man sits down next to her and says, "Hey, this is supposed to be a bar for boxing fans."

"Are you kidding? I'm the biggest boxing fan in the world."

"You are?" says the man, happy to find a woman who shares his interests.

"Why, I'm such a big boxing fan," she continues, "that I have a tattoo of Mike Tyson on one thigh and a tattoo of Evander Holyfeld on the other. Wanna see them?"

"Sure," says the man, downing his scotch.

The woman hikes up her skirt, spreads her legs, and grabs the man's head and shoves it down there. "Can you see Iron Mike? Can you see Evander?" she asks.

The man comes up for air and says, "Yeah, I saw them both, but you didn't say you had Don King in the middle."

>> Dole was asked the presidential underwear question: boxers or briefs?

After a moment's reflection, he answered, "Depends . . . "

>> Q: How many right-to-lifers does it take to change a lightbulb?

A: Two. One to change the lightbulb, and one to proclaim that life began at the screwing.

>> A husband and wife were driving down the highway. Coming in the opposite direction was Lorena Bobbitt. She had just cut off John's penis. As she passed the husband and wife, she threw John's penis out the window of her car and it hit the windshield of the oncoming car. The husband turned to his wife and said, "Honey, did you see the size of the dick on that bug?"

>> Q: How does Bill Clinton say "fuck you"?

A: "Trust me."

>> Q: What is the difference between Dan Quayle, Bill Clinton, and Jane Fonda?

A: Jane Fonda went to Vietnam.

>> Q: How did Bill and Hillary Clinton meet?

A: They were dating the same girl in high school.

>> Q: What are Bill's two favorite campaign promises?

A: "The check is in your mouth," and, "I won't come in the mail."

>> Q: Why did Bill and Hillary send Chelsea to a private school?

A: If they sent her to a public school, the secret service would be outgunned.

>> Q: Did you hear Chrysler is introducing a new car to commemorate President Clinton's election?

A: It's gonna be called the Dodge Drafter.

>> Q: What do you get when you cross a crooked lawyer with a crooked politician?

A: Chelsea.

>> Q: What famous Arkansas State Supreme Court decision did Hillary Clinton fight for?

A: If you divorce your wife in Arkansas, she is still your cousin.

>> Q: Why is Chelsea Clinton a miracle child?

A: Because lawyers use their personalities for birth control.

>> Q: What does Bill say to Hillary after having sex?

A: I'll be home in fifteen minutes.

>> A sign at a Clinton rally: Smoke Dope. Dodge the draft. Cheat on your wife. Become President. It's the American dream.

>> When Bill and Hillary were engaged, he discovered she was a virgin. Immediately he called his mother in Arkansas to say he thought he should call the wedding off.

"How come, son?" his mom asked.

Bill replied, "I just figure if she ain't good enough for her own kinfolk, she ain't good enough for ours."

>> Q: Why did Arnold Schwarzenegger and Maria Shriver get married?

A: They're trying to breed a bulletproof Kennedy.

>> Did you hear that Jeff Smith, the "Frugal Gourmet," after being accused of trying to seduce teenage boys, announced that he was leaving the television series. Around the same time, Michael Jackson announced the hiring of a new chef at his Neverland Ranch.

>> Q: Why did Mike Tyson learn to bite ears?

A: How else do you tell a 275-pound inmate that "no means no"?

>> A confused nine-year-old boy goes up to his mother and asks, "Is God male or female?"

After thinking a moment, his mother responds, "Well, God is both male and female."

This confuses the little boy, so he asks, "Is God black or white?"

"Well, God is both black and white."

This further confuses the boy, so he asks, "Is God gay or straight?"

At this the mother is getting concerned, but answers nonetheless, "Honey, God is both gay and straight."

At this, the boy's face lights up with understanding, and he triumphantly asks, "Is God Michael Jackson?"

5

Visualize This!

FUNNY HOW THINGS can be funny at the time. Alice's mother, the late Fonzo, once cracked up the whole family when a meat grinder broke and she asked her brother-in-law to fix it. She kept trying to tell him how to do it and in her eagerness shouted, "Fred! Fred! Pull that liver."

For years afterward, any time anyone in the family used the word "lever," someone inevitably would shout out, "Fred! Fred! Pull that liver." Suddenly everyone would be guffawing away, tears rolling down their cheeks, and Fonzo would be running to the bathroom before she sprang a leak.

It's part of family lore. It's a joke. And most importantly, it conjures up a great picture of Uncle Fred pulling on his liver in the kitchen.

Even in the forties, when life was "clean," a good joke that forced you to imagine something obscene was appreciated and considered "family" entertainment.

Why are such jokes funny? Much like a flasher, the power of a joke is in the surprise.

Our genitals are not particularly amusing to look at, but if you saw them on the front page of *The New York Times* tomorrow, you'd probably have yourself a good old chuckle.

Visualization jokes are like post-hypnotic suggestions. They force you to do things with your mind you hadn't intended, indeed, that you do not have conscious control over. You are not responsible. You can say to yourself as you're visualizing the most obscene things: "I didn't want to think dirty. They made me."

It's like the old motel wall plaque with the drawing of a little boy in a weighted-down diaper labeled: The Devil Made Me Do It.

The primitive version of this intellectual process is flashing or mooning or streaking—which attempt to evoke the sudden gone-out-of-control feeling that comes with forced exposure to the naked body, especially the verboten zones.

Since we are in the print medium here, dear reader, you must supply the pictures. We realize our awesome responsibility not to slip any unpleasant images on you. So we have eliminated any dirty jokes that force the reader to picture something more disgusting than either of us could stand—which eliminated three jokes.

There were disagreements among the authors on which visuals crossed the line from funny to tasteless. We discovered much about our selves in this process. Hidden aspects of our personalities were revealed. And the important thing we learned here is that men love cunt jokes and women don't.

As a warm-up to this section, we ask the reader to perform the following exercise. And we mean it! You think we're fucking joking here? This is serious business. Do not enter the following section without obeying our instructions exactly. We take no responsibility for readers who have not consulted their physician before beginning. This shit really works, folks. Now, begin:

1. Retire to a quiet peaceful place (bathroom, bedroom closet, whatever. . .).

2. Put on some soft gentle music (BeeGees, Chopin, Erik Satie, but *no Kenny G.*).

3. Close your eyes and begin breathing slowly, rhythmically, and with an emphasis on exhalation (you know: in/*out*, in/*out*, in/*out*. . .).

4. Now start panting. Start moaning. Start saying, "Yes! Yes! Yesssss!"

5a. Now imagine a woman's vagina singing to you (straight male and lesbian version).

5b. Now imagine an erect penis shouting, "Honey, I'm home" (straight female and gay male version).

5c. Now imagine your boss on the toilet (asexual worka-holic version).

6. Now visualize world peace.

>> SUBJECT: Visualize This!

>> Three cowboys are sitting around a campfire, way out on the range, telling the tall tales of bravado that are part of cowboy lore.

The first says, "I must be the meanest, toughest cowboy there is. Why, just the other day, a bull got loose in the corral and gored ten men before I wres-tled it to the ground by the horns with my bare hands."

The second couldn't stand to be outdone. "Why that's nothing. I was walking down the trail yesterday, and a fifteen-foot rattler slid out from under a rock and came at me. I grabbed that snake with my bare hands, bit its head off, and sucked the poison down in one gulp. And I'm still here today."

The third cowboy remained silent, slowly stirring the coals with his penis.

>> A husband and wife love to golf together, but neither of them is playing well, so they decide to take private lessons.

The husband has his lesson first. After the pro sees his swing, he says, "No, no, no. You're gripping the club way too hard."

"Well, what should I do?" asks the man.

"Hold the club gently," the pro replies, "just like you'd hold your wife's breast."

The man takes the advice, takes a swing, and wow! He hits the ball 250 yards, straight up the fairway.

The man goes back to his wife with the good news, and the wife can't wait for her lesson.

The next day the wife goes for her lesson. The pro watches her swing and says, "No, no, no. You're gripping the club way too hard."

"What can I do?" asks the wife.

"Hold the club gently, just like you'd hold your husband's penis." The wife listens carefully to the pro's advice, takes a swing, and thump. The ball goes straight down the fairway, about fifteen feet.

"That was great," the pro says, "nice and gentle. Now take the club out of your mouth and swing it with your hands!"

>> Three old men lived in a senior citizen's complex, and they were always bored because smoking, drinking, card playing, and all fun was forbidden. Then one day they found some amusement. They found Ethel, an old lady who now and then held their "things" in

her hand. For the service they gave her their coffee money. Some time later Ethel said "Hi boys. I haven't seen you for a while."

The men replied, "We've been on the third floor in Mary's room."

Ethel was offended. "What does Mary have that I don't have?"

The men answered, "Parkinson's disease."

>> Jack goes to the doctor and says, "Doc, I'm having trouble getting my penis erect. Can you help me?"

After a complete examination the doctor tells Jack, "Well, the problem with you is that the muscles around the base of your penis are damaged. There's really nothing I can do for you, unless you're willing to try an experimental treatment."

Jack asks sadly, "What is this treatment?"

"Well," the doctor explains, "what we would do is take the muscles from the trunk of a baby elephant and implant them in your penis."

Jack thinks about it silently then says, "Well, the thought of going through life without ever having sex again is too much. Let's go for it."

A few weeks after the operation, Jack was given the green light to use his improved equipment. He planned a romantic evening for his girlfriend and took her to one of the nicest restaurants in the city. In the middle of dinner, he felt a stirring between his legs that continued to the point of being painful. To release the pressure Jack unzipped his fly. His penis immediately sprang from his pants, went to the top of the table, grabbed a roll, and then returned to his pants. His girlfriend was stunned at first, but then said with a sly smile, "That was incredible. Can you do it again?"

Jack replied with his eyes watering, "Well, I guess so, but I don't think I can fit another roll up my ass."

>> A handicapped Vietnam veteran is limping down the street, dragging his right foot along behind him. He looks up and sees another guy about his age walking toward him. This guy is also dragging his right foot along behind him. Another disabled Joe! The 'Nam vet walks up to him, grabs him by the hand and says, "Mekong Delta, 1969."

The other guy looks him square in the face and says, "Dog shit, five minutes ago."

>> A little old lady walked into the main branch of Chase Manhattan Bank holding a large paper bag in her hand. She told the young man at the window that she wished to open an account with the bank and deposit the $3 million she had in the bag. She said that prior to doing so she wished to meet the president of the bank, due to the large amount of money involved. The teller opened the bag and saw bundles of $100 bills. Thinking her request was reasonable, he telephoned the president's secretary to make an appointment for the lady.

Later, the lady was escorted upstairs and ushered into the president's office. Introductions were made, and she stated that she liked to get to know the people she did business with on a more personal level. The bank president then asked her how she came into such a large sum of money and whether it was perhaps an inheritance. She replied "No, I bet on people." Seeing his confusion, she explained that she just bet different things with different people. All of a sudden she said, "I'll bet you $25,000 that by 10 AM tomorrow morning your balls will be square." The bank president figured that she must be off her rocker but decided to take her up on the bet. He didn't see how he could lose.

For the rest of the day, he was very careful. He decided to stay home that evening and take no chances. After all, $25,000 was at stake. When he got up in the morning and took his shower, he checked to make sure everything was normal. There was no difference. He looked the same as he always had. He went to work, humming as he went, and waited for the little old lady to come in at ten. He knew that this would be a good day. How often do you get handed $25,000 for doing nothing, he thought.

At 10 AM sharp, the little old lady was shown into the president's office. With her was a younger man she introduced as her lawyer. She said she always took him along whenever there was this much money involved. "Well," she asked, "what about our bet?"

"I don't know how to tell you this," he replied, "but I'm the same as I've always been, only $25,000 richer." The little old lady seemed to accept this but insisted that she be able to see for herself. The bank president thought the request reasonable and dropped his trousers. She instructed him to bend over and then she grabbed hold of him. Sure enough, everything was fine, but then the bank president looked up and saw the lady's attorney across the room, banging his head against the wall.

"What's wrong with him?" he asked.

"Oh, him?" she replied. "I bet him $100,000 that by 10 AM this morning I'd have the president of the Chase Manhattan Bank by the balls."

>> This man and his wife decide to move from the city to the country, so they buy a small farm and move. A while later they decide they need some animals for their farm, so the man goes into the local village market the next day. He's walking around and spots a farmer selling roosters. He decides that a rooster would be good on his little farm. The farmer, seeing the city man coming along, decides here is a way to make extra money on the stupid city guy. The man asks the farmer how much for a rooster, to which the farmer replies, "Oh no, these aren't roosters, these are special. They are known as cocks, and they are much better than roosters. A cock will protect your farm—unlike a rooster." So the city guy thinks he is getting a good deal and pays a bit extra for the cock.

So the guy walks along carrying his cock, and he comes upon a farmer selling hens. This farmer seeing that he is a city guy, decides that he can also make a bit of extra cash. The man asks how much for a hen to which this farmer replies, "Oh no, these aren't normal hens. These are known as pullets, and they will lay twice as many eggs as a hen." So once again the guy falls for it and pays a little extra.

So he's walking along carrying his purchases under his arms, when he sees a guy selling donkeys. He has always wanted a donkey. But once again, this farmer knows he can make some extra money off of a stupid city guy, so when the man asks how much for a donkey, the farmer replies, "This is not a donkey. This is an ass. A donkey will stop walking, and you won't get him started again. But if an ass stops walking, all you have to do is scratch him on his back, and he will start walking again." So of course the man pays extra for the ass.

So he's riding his ass home, when all of a sudden it stops, but he has his two chickens under his arms and can't get him to move. So along comes one of the village ladies and the man yells out to her, "Excuse me, can you do me a favor?"

"Of course," says the lady, "anything for a nice man from the city. What is it?"

To which the city man replies, "Can you please hold my cock and pullet while I scratch my ass?"

>> A guy goes into a store and asks the cashier—a horny young woman with the body of a goddess but the head of a pit bull—for some rubbers. The cashier asks, "What size?"

The guy replies, "Size? I didn't know they came in sizes."

"Yes, they do," she says. "What size do you want?"

"Got no idea," the guy answers.

The woman is used to this, so she tells him to go to the backyard and measure himself by sticking his penis into each of the three holes in the fence. While the man is back there, the woman sneaks around to the other side of the fence and positions herself behind each hole as the man tests it.

When they return, the woman asks, "What will it be—small, medium, or large?"

The guy replies, "To hell with the rubbers. How much for the fence!"

>> Tarzan has been living alone in his jungle kingdom for thirty years, with only apes for company and suitably shaped holes in trees for sex, when Jane, a reporter, comes to Africa in search of this legendary figure.

Deep in the jungle, she comes into a clearing to discover Tarzan thrusting vigorously into a hole in the jungle oak. Overcome by this display of animal passion, Jane makes herself known to Tarzan and offers herself to him. As she reclines naked on the grass, Tarzan takes a run up and then gives her a huge boot in the crotch. She screams at him, "What the hell did you do that for?"

Tarzan replies, "Always check for squirrels."

>> Seems there was a treasure ship on its way back to port. About halfway there, it was approached by a pirate ship with its skull and crossbones waving in the breeze.

"Captain, Captain, what do we do?" asked the first mate.

"First Mate," said the captain, "go to my cabin, open my sea chest, and bring me my red shirt." The first mate did so.

Wearing his bright red shirt, the captain exhorted his crew to fight. So inspiring was he, in fact, that the pirate ship was repelled without casualties.

A few days later, the ship was again approached, this time by two pirate sloops.

"Captain, Captain, what should we do?"

"First Mate, bring me my red shirt!"

The crew, emboldened by their fearless captain, fought heroically, and managed to defeat both boarding parties, though they took many casualties. That night, the survivors had a great celebration. The first mate asked the captain the secret of his bright red shirt.

"It's simple, First Mate. If I am wounded, the blood does not show, and the crew continues to fight without fear."

A week passed, and they were nearing their home port, when suddenly the lookout cried that ten ships of the enemy's armada were approaching.

"Captain, Captain, we're in terrible trouble. What do we do?" The first mate looked expectantly at the miracle worker.

Pale with fear, the captain commanded, "First Mate, bring me my brown pants."

>> An old man of seventy married a young girl of eighteen. When they got into bed the night after the wedding, he held up three fingers.

"Oh, honey," said the young nymph. "Does that mean we're going to do it three times?"

"No," said the old man. "It means you can take your pick."

>> A little boy gets up to go to the bathroom in the middle of the night. As he passes his parents' bedroom, he peeks in through the keyhole. He watches for a moment, then continues on down the hallway, saying to himself, "Boy, and she gets mad at me for sucking my thumb."

>> A woman walks into a bar totally nude and asks the barkeep if he can serve her a drink. He looks her up and down and says, "Well sure, but you don't look like you'll be able to pay for it."

The woman throws one leg up on a bar stool and shows what she's got. "Will this do?" she asks.

The barkeep takes a look and responds, "Ya got anything smaller?"

>> A famous hypnotist was performing in a large auditorium full of people one night. He began to speak in a soft and steady voice over the loudspeaker system. "Listen to the sound of my voice. . . ." he kept repeating "The sound of my voice . . . every word is a command . . . the sound of my voice . . ."

Pretty soon, he had every single person in the audience completely mesmerized, each one hanging on his every word.

Needing to take a quick piss, he announced, "I will have to leave the stage for a moment, but you will all remain in a trance while I am gone." And then he repeated the words, "The sound of my voice . . . every word is a command." As he turned to go, he tripped over the microphone cord, landed on his ass, and yelled, "Shit!"

≫ A farmer went into town for market day and sold everything but a small goose. Afterward, he decided to go see a movie while in town. At the movie theater, the ticket girl took one look at the goose and said, "You can't take the bird inside, mister." The farmer went around the corner, stuck the bird under his coveralls, and headed back to the theater. During the movie, the goose started getting restless, so the farmer unzipped his fly so the bird could stick his head out for some fresh air.

Sitting next to the farmer were two little old ladies. One turned to the other, whispering, "Minnie, I thought when you'd seen one, you'd seen 'em all, but I'll be damned if the one on the guy next to me ain't eating my popcorn."

≫ Q: Why does Helen Keller need two hands to masturbate?

A: One to do the work and the other to moan with.

≫ This guy was walking through the zoo one day. When he was in front of the gorilla cage, he bent down to tie his shoe. He noticed through the corner of his eye that the gorilla had also bent down. Then when he stood back up he saw that the gorilla also stood back up. To see if it was a coincidence, he bent down to tie his other shoe, and once again the gorilla bent down. He stood up, and the gorilla stood up. After glancing over his shoulder to make sure that nobody else was around, the man jumped up in the air. And you guessed it: The gorilla jumped up. The man was getting a kick out of it. He started making faces at the gorilla, and the gorilla would copy everything he did. Finally the man got next to the cage and pulled the lower lid of his right eye down. At this point the gorilla reached through the cage, grabbed the guy by the collar, and banged him against the bars ferociously. After hearing all the commotion, the zookeeper came running over to the man. "What on earth happened?" asked the zookeeper.

"I don't know" said the man. "He seemed calm a second ago. I was jumping around and he was jumping around and he was doing every thing I was doing. Then all of a sudden, after I pulled my lower eyelid down, he got all mad and beat the hell out of me."

"Well, no wonder!" exclaimed the zookeeper. "That means 'fuck you' in gorilla talk."

"Oh," said the man, not quite satisfied. He left the zoo but returned an hour later with a large shopping bag. Again, after making sure that no one was watching, he started jumping around and the gorilla did the same. After a minute or two of this he grabbed the bag and pulled out two butcher knives and threw one of them into the cage. He lifted the other knife over his head, at which point the gorilla grabbed his knife and also lifted it over his head. After a minute of cutting the air with his knife and watching the gorilla do likewise, the man snuck a large salami out of the bag with his other hand and stuck it between his legs. With a sweeping motion he came down with the knife and whacked off the salami: Whack.

At this, the gorilla simply looked at the man and pulled down his lower eyelid.

>> Q: What do you get when you cross Raggedy Ann with the Pillsbury doughboy?

A: A redhead with a yeast infection.

>> A man and a woman are riding next to each other in first class. The man sneezes, pulls out his wang and wipes the tip off.

The woman can't believe what she just saw and decides she is hallucinating. A few minutes pass. The man sneezes again. He pulls out his wang and wipes the tip off. The woman is about to go nuts. She can't believe that such a rude person exists. A few minutes pass. The man sneezes yet again. He takes his wang out and wipes the tip off. The woman has finally had enough. She turns to the man and says, "Three times you've sneezed, and three times you've removed your penis from your pants to wipe it off. What the hell kind of degenerate are you?"

The man replies, "I am sorry to have disturbed you, ma'am. I have a very rare condition such that when I sneeze, I have an orgasm."

The woman, taken aback, then says, "Oh, how strange. What are you taking for it?"

The man looks at her and says, "Pepper."

>> An attractive woman from New York was driving through a remote part of Texas when her car broke down. An Indian on horseback came along and offered her a ride to a nearby town. She climbed up behind him on the horse, and they rode off. The ride was uneventful except that every few minutes the Indian would let out a whoop so loud that it would echo from the surrounding hills.

When they arrived in town, he let her off at the local service station, yelled one final, "Yahoo!" and rode off.

"What did you do to get that Indian so excited?" asked the service-station attendant.

"Nothing. I merely sat behind him on the horse, put my arms around his waist, and held onto his saddle horn so I wouldn't fall off."

"Lady," the attendant said, "Indians ride bareback."

>> A boy sees his mother naked, coming out of the shower. He points at her pussy and asks, "What's that?"

"That's my black sponge," his embarrassed mother answers.

Later the boy spills a glass of milk and comes running to his mother. "Can I use your black sponge?" he asks.

"Oh I'm sorry. I lost it somewhere. Here take this paper towel," his mother replies.

Later that day he comes running to his mother and shouts, "Mama, Mama, I found your black sponge!"

Amazed, the mother asks the boy where it is.

The boy answers, "It's next door at Mrs. Johnson's house, and Daddy's washing his face with it."

Cum As
You Are:
alt·sex·cum
and
perv·sex·cum

ALTERNATIVE SEX IS THE SEX people have when there is no alternative. What the Internet calls alternative can be a biological inevitability, a conditioned reflex, or just what you do because Meg Ryan is not available.

Of course this alternative designation is totally arbitrary. A woman having intercourse with a man is norm.sex. A man having intercourse with a man is alt.sex. A man having intercourse with a sheep is perv.sex, and a sheep having intercourse with a sheep is animal husbandry.

In organizing these sections we are going according to the San Francisco Bay Area Rules of Order. Alt.sex includes lesbian, homosexual, S & M, and A & W—which is doing it with a root beer. (Don't try this at home, kids.)

The category of sex that goes beyond the alt norms we call perv.sex. Despite objections from Michael Jackson's lawyers, we have deemed sex with children and animals to be perverted rather than just alternative. This is the '90s. Whatever turns you on will not do. It must be adult and human.

One man's alt.sex is another woman's normal sheep shagging. The point is we use the Internet user-group term "alt," meaning alternative, to refer to gay sex jokes because that is Internet convention. However, we recognize that alt.sex is only alt to the straight world, and in the gay world it's yummy.sex. Other popular user groups:

1. alt.cocker.sex: old people's sex
2. alt.titude.sex: mile high club

3. norm.sex: sex with the guy at the bar on *Cheers*
4. chicken.sex: sex when you're scared
5. alt.chicken.sex: sex in Arkansas
6. sick.sex: sex with chicken soup
7. homo.sex.url: San Francisco sex
8. sex.$$$.cum: New York sex
9. ego.sex: L.A. sex
10. Microsoft.sex: fucking the competition.

So what's so funny about someone doing it differently than you? First of all, sex is funny. As Sam Johnson or maybe Woody Allen said: The pleasure is momentary, the cost tremendous, and the position ridiculous.

It's that position stuff that really sets sex apart from eating dinner or watching TV or brushing your teeth. You don't stick a pork chop in your private parts. You don't put the remote between your legs. You don't suck the toothbrush, but in sex all sorts of weird positions and permutations come into play.

OK, let's say you do suck the toothbrush. Let's say you do put the pork chop up your ass. Better yet, let's say you suck the pork chop and put it up your partner's ass. Now hit the remote and brush your teeth with the pork chop. It doesn't get any more alt than this, folks.

But what is funny about perv sex? What is so darned funny when Lenny Bruce says, "When you're lying in bed with a chick or a chicken. . ."? It's basically a guy thing. Men will—as we all know—fuck anything: their wives, Marla Maples, a chicken. You don't hear a lot of women-fucking-animals jokes. This is because women have taste. They'd only fuck a chicken if it had a lot of money.

But no one finds sex with children funny. When Michael Jackson is caught red-handed and says things like "I just had three naked boys in the hot tub to play bobbing for apples," we are not amused.

Well, maybe a little. . .

>> SUBJECT: Cum As You Are

A. Alt.sex.cum (I Can Get My Behind Where You're Coming From)

>> There once was a man named Penis Van Lesbian, who very much wanted to be an actor. Even though he was good at what he did, people kept turning him down at his auditions, for they found his name would be too offensive to advertise. Penis Van Lesbian finally decided to get an agent, who told him the only way he'd get any roles was to change his name . . . so they changed it to Dick Van Dyke.

>> Two gay guys decide that they want to have a baby, but they don't want to adopt because they want the baby to be as close to their own as possible. So they both masturbate into a cup and have a doctor use their sperm to impregnate a female friend of theirs. Nine months later, the two gay guys are looking at their baby in the hospital nursery. All of the babies are crying and screaming except for theirs.

"Wow," one of the gay guys says, "Our baby is the most well behaved one in here."

A nurse who happens to be walking by says, "Now he's quiet, but wait till we take the pacifier out of his ass."

>> A flying saucer lands in a couple's backyard, and a male and female alien emerge from the ship. The alien couple take a look at the humans and propose an evening of mate swapping. The curious humans quickly agree.

That night, the wife is with the male alien. He undresses and she stares at his perfect body. Then her gaze crosses his groin, and a look of disappointment comes over her.

"Is there something wrong?" asks the alien.

"Well, you seem so . . . uh . . . small."

"No problem," replies the alien. He twists his ear and his organ grows longer. The woman still seems disappointed.

She indicates she would like the alien to be wider. He twists the other ear and grows wider.

The next morning over breakfast, the wife tells her husband what a wonderful night she had with the alien and that she can hardly wait to share some of the techniques with her husband the next night. "Honey, how was your night?" she asks.

"Terrible," he said. "The female alien was truly beautiful, but all night long all she did was twist my ears!"

>> A young guy goes into a bar, notices two foxy blondes sitting at the end of the bar. He tells the bartender, "I'd like to buy those two ladies a drink."

The bartender says, "It's your money, bud, but they're lesbians."

"What's a lesbian?" the guy asks.

The bartender answers, "Why don't you go over there and ask them?"

So the young guy walks over to the women and says, "The bartender says you girls are lesbians. What's that?"

One of the girls answers politely, "Well, we like to kiss and fondle each others breasts."

The guy yells back to the bartender, "Hey, we need three drinks over here for us lesbians."

>> Q: Name two famous people who were shot in the back of the head?

A. JFK and the guy in the movie theater sitting in front of Pee Wee Herman.

>> Q: What do you call a lesbian with long fingers?

A: Well hung.

>> A nun got into a cab, and the driver was staring at her. She asked him why was he staring at her, and he said, "I want to ask you a question, but I don't want to offend you."

She said, "You can't offend me, not as old as I am and as long as I have been a nun. I've heard just about everything."

The cabdriver said, "Well, I've always had a fantasy to have a nun give me a blow job."

She said, "Well let's see what we can work out. I have two conditions: One—you have to be single. Two—you have to be Catholic."

The cabdriver said, "Oh I'm single and I am Catholic."

She said, "OK, pull in to the alley," and he did. So she did her thing. Then they were on the street again.

Suddenly the cabdriver started laughing, and the nun said, "My child, what's so funny?"

He said, "Ha ha, I pulled a fast one on you, sister. The truth is I'm married, and I'm Jewish!"

She said, "That's OK. My name is Steve, and I'm on my way to a costume party."

>> Q: How did Melissa Etheridge drown?

A: They found her face down in Ricki Lake.

>> Q: What do you call a gay dinosaur?

A: Megasoreass.

>> Q: What do you call a lesbian dinosaur?

A: Licalottapuss.

>> Steve has been shopping for a new motorcycle. He finally finds one for a great price, but it's missing a seal, so whenever it rains he has to smear Vaseline over the spot where the seal should be.

Anyway, his girlfriend is having him over for dinner to meet her parents. He drives his new bike to her house, where she is outside waiting for him. "No matter what happens at dinner tonight, don't say a word," she tells him. "Our family had a fight a while ago about doing dishes. We haven't done any since, but the first person to speak at dinner has to do them."

Steve sits down for dinner, and it is just how she described it. Dishes are piled up to the ceiling in the kitchen, and nobody is saying a word. So Steve decides to have a little fun. He grabs his girlfriend, throws her on the table, and has sex with her in front of her parents. His girlfriend is a little flustered, her dad is obviously livid, and her mom horrified when he sits back down—but no one says a word.

A few minutes later he grabs her mom, throws her on the table, and does a repeat performance. Now his girlfriend is furious, her dad is boiling, and her mother is a little happier—but still there is complete silence at the table.

All of a sudden there is a loud clap of thunder, and it starts to rain. Steve remembers his motorcycle. He jumps up and grabs his jar of Vaseline. Upon witnessing this, his girlfriend's father backs away from the table and screams:

"OK, enough already, I'll do the fucking dishes!"

>> A man walks into a public men's room, his arms held out to his sides, hands hanging limply down, with his fingers spread stiffly apart. He approaches another man and asks, "Could you please unzip my fly?" The second man, figuring the other guy must be crippled, is very embarrassed, but complies. His embarrassment grows as the man next asks him to pull out his penis and hold it while the man pees.

After the first guy finishes, the second man starts to put the guy's penis back into his pants.

"Oh, I can take care of that," says the first man, blowing on his fingers. "I think my nails are dry now."

>> The traveling salesman's car broke down in the country and he knocked on the farmhouse door. When the farmer opened the door, the salesman said, "Sir, my car has broken down, and I was wondering if you might be able to put me up for the night?"

The farmer said, "Why, sure, but you will have to sleep with my son."

The salesman hesitated then said, "Excuse me, sir, but I think I'm in the wrong joke."

>> Three young candidates for the priesthood are told by the monsignor they have to pass one more test: The Celibacy Test. The monsignor leads them into a room, tells them to undress, and a small bell is tied to each man's penis. In comes a beautiful woman, wearing a sexy belly-dancer costume. She begins to dance sensually around the first candidate.

Ting-a-ling, the bell sounds.

"Oh, Patrick," says the monsignor, "I am so disappointed in your lack of control. Go take a long, cold shower and pray about your carnal weakness." The candidate leaves.

The dancer continues, dancing around the second candidate, slowly peeling off her layers of veils. As the last veil drops:

Ting-a-ling, the bell sounds.

"Joseph, Joseph," sighs the monsignor. "You too are unable to withstand your carnal desires. Go take a long, cold shower and pray for forgiveness."

The dancer continues, dancing naked in front of the final candidate. Nothing. She writhes up and down against his body. No response. Finally, exhausted, she quits.

"Michael, my son, I am truly proud of you," says the Monsignor. "Only you have the true strength of character needed to become a priest. Now, go and join your weaker brethren in the showers."

And from the other room, the monsignor hears: *Ting-a-ling*.

>> First guy: Hey, if you went camping with another guy and woke up with Vaseline on your butt hole, would you tell anyone?

Second guy: Hell no!

First guy: Wanna go camping?

>> A woman walks into a sex shop and asks the clerk, "D-d-do y-y-you s-s-s-ell v-v-vibrators?"

The clerk replies, "Yes, ma'am."

The woman asks, "Th-th-th-the r-r-r-eally b-b-b-ig o-o-nes?"

The clerk replies, "Yes, ma'am."

The woman asks, "Th-th-th-the o-o-o-nes w-w-w-ith t-t-t-he t-t-two s-s-speed s-s-witch?"

The clerk replies, "Yes, ma'am . . . right here."

The woman asks, "C-c-c-c-can y-y-you t-t-tell m-mm-me h-how t-t-to t-t-turn t-t-them o-o-off?"

B. Perv.sex.cum (I Can Get My Chicken's Behind Where You're Coming From)

>> As she lay there dozing next to me, a voice inside my head kept saying, "Relax. You're not the first doctor to sleep with one of his patients."

But another voice kept reminding me, "Howard, you're a veterinarian."

>> A guy goes bear hunting. He sees a bear in the distance and fires his bear rifle at it. The bear, wounded just slightly, is very angry and runs up to the hunter and screams at him, "How dare you try to kill me. I ought to just kill you, but I'll give you one chance to show you're sorry and save your life. Kneel down and give me a blow job." After the man gives the bear the blow job, the bear warns him not to do any more bear hunting.

The next day, though, the guy shows up in the woods again with his bear rifle. Again the guy spots the bear and fires on him, but he misses. The bear runs up to the guy and yells, "This time I'm really going to teach you a lesson," and proceeds to buttfuck the guy several times. The guy is exhausted on the ground, and the bear leaves with a warning, "Just lay off the goddamn bear hunting, OK?"

But the next day the guy shows up in the woods again carrying his bear rifle. The bear runs right up to the guy and asks, "You're not here for the hunting, are you?"

>> This guy pulls into his driveway after a long day at work to find all his belongings out in the front yard. He enters his house and asks his girlfriend, "What's going on?"

She says, "I found out you're a pedophile, and I want you to leave."

He looks at her and says, "Pedophile, huh? That's a pretty big word for a ten year old."

>> A guy was out in his backyard one day when he looked over toward his neighbors and saw that the guy was fucking a goat. The man was shocked and went inside and called the police. The neighbor was arrested.

After getting out on bail, the arrested man called one of his friends and explained the situation, asking for suggestions on getting some legal help. "Well, I know a couple good attorneys. The first one is really fantastic, has won every case, but he's expensive and I don't think you could afford him. But the other guy is pretty good, too. He wins most of his cases, and I think he's in your budget. The amazing thing about this guy is his knack of picking a jury. In fact, that's where I'm sure all his cases have been won."

So our friend hires the second lawyer, and they go to court. The first witness is his neighbor, who is called upon to describe what he saw.

"Well, it was about 1:30 in the afternoon, and I was in my backyard. I looked over into the yard next door and saw the defendant performing the sex act with a goat. As he finished, the goat turned around and licked him."

In the box, a member of the jury nudges the guy next to him and says, "You know, a good goat'll do that."

>> Two drunks are sitting in the gutter watching a dog lick his private parts. One says to the other "Gee, I wish I could do that."

The other says, "Better pet him first."

>> A new guy in town walks into a bar and reads a sign that hangs over the bar: FREE BEER FOR THE PERSON WHO CAN PASS THE TEST! So the guy asks the bartender what the test is.

The bartender says, "Well, first you have to drink that whole gallon of pepper tequila, the whole thing at once. And you can't make a face while doing it. Second, there's a 'gator out back with a sore tooth. You have to remove it with your bare hands. Third, there's a woman upstairs who's never had an orgasm. You gotta make things right for her."

The man says, "Well, as much as I would love free beer, I won't do it."

As time goes on and the man drinks a few, he asks, "Wherez zat teeqeelah?" He grabs the gallon of tequila with both hands and downs it with a big slurp, tears streaming down his face.

Next he staggers out back, and soon all the people inside hear the most frightening roaring and thumping, then silence.

The man staggers back into the bar, his shirt ripped and big scratches all over his body.

"Now," he says, "Where's that woman with the sore tooth?"

>> "Make it a double, Joe," the dejected man told the bartender. "I just got the shock of my life. I caught my wife screwing my best friend."

"Paul, that's awful. What did you do?"

"I hit him in the nose with a newspaper and sent him to bed with no Kibbles 'N' Bits."

>> The Seven Dwarfs go to a convent and ask to speak to the mother superior. They are led into her office and Doc immediately asks, "Is there a two-foot-tall nun in this convent?"

"No, my son," replies the mother superior.

Then Sleepy asks, "Is there a two-foot nun in this country?"

"I'm afraid not," comes the reply.

Sneezy then asks, "Is there a two-foot nun in the whole world?"

"No," says the mother superior.

Six of the dwarfs then start chanting: "Grumpy shagged a penguin."

>> Two ladies brought their dogs to the vet; one had a Great Dane and the other had a little poodle, both males. The lady with the Great Dane asked the lady with the poodle why she brought her dog in, and she replied, "Oh, it's so embarrassing. My little Snookums humps everyone and everything, so I've come to get him neutered."

The lady with the Great Dane replied, "I know what you mean. My dog does the same thing. Every time I bend over, he jumps up behind me and starts humping away."

The lady with the poodle said, "Then I guess you're here to get your dog neutered too."

"No," the lady with the Great Dane replied, "just to get his nails trimmed."

>> There is a new commander on a base of the French Foreign Legion and the captain is showing him around all the buildings. After they've made the rounds, the commander looks at the captain and says, "Wait a minute. You haven't shown me that small blue building over there. What's that used for?"

The captain says, "Well sir, you see that there are no women around. Whenever the men feel the need for a woman, they go there and use the camel."

"Enough!" says the commander in disgust.

Well, two weeks later, the commander himself starts to feel in need of a woman. He goes to the captain and says, "Tell me something, Captain." Lowering his voice and glancing around, he asks, "Is the camel free any time soon?"

The captain says, "Well, let me see." He opens up his book. "Why, yes, sir, the camel is free tomorrow afternoon at two o'clock."

The commander says, "Put me down for two o'clock then."

So the next day at two o'clock the commander goes to the little blue building and opens the door. There inside he finds the cutest camel he's ever seen. Right next to the camel is a little step stool, so he closes the door behind him and puts the step stool directly behind the camel. He stands on the stool, drops his pants, and begins to have sex with the camel. A minute later the captain walks in.

"Ahem, begging your pardon, sir," says the captain, "but wouldn't it be wiser to ride the camel into town and find a woman like the other men?"

>> An old guy is sitting on a bus when a punk rocker gets on. The punk rocker's hair is red, green, yellow, and orange. He has feather earrings.

When he sees the old man staring at him, the punk rocker says "What's the matter old man? Didn't you ever do anything wild when you were a young guy?"

The old guy says in reply, "Yeah. One time I fucked a parrot. I thought maybe you were my kid."

>> A farmer was worried that none of his pigs were getting pregnant. He called a vet and asked what he should do if he wanted more pigs. The vet told him he should try artificial insemination.

The farmer, not wanting to appear stupid, answered "OK" and hung up the phone. Unclear on what the vet meant by artificial insemination, the farmer decided it must mean he had to impregnate the pigs himself, so he loaded all the pigs in his pickup and drove down to the woods and shagged them all.

The next day he called the vet again and asked how he would know if the pigs were pregnant. The vet told him they would be lying down rolling in the mud, but when he looked out the window not even one was lying down. So, he loaded them up in his pickup again and drove them to the woods and shagged them all again.

To his dismay they were all standing the next morning. So, again he loaded the pigs in his truck, drove them to the woods, and shagged them for the third time.

By the next morning the farmer was beat, so he asked his wife to hop out of bed and look out the window to see what the pigs were doing. She said "Hmmm—that's weird. They're all in the truck, and one of them is blowing the horn."

>> After a hard day at the office, three guys decide to go out for a cocktail to wind down. The bar becomes very crowded. A few drinks turn into many, and soon everyone is tanked. All three lose track of each other and end up going home separately.

The next day at the office, the three gather by the water cooler to discuss the past evening's events. The first guy says, "I got so drunk last night that I went home and blew chunks."

The second guy pipes in, "That's nothing. I got so drunk that I got in my car and drove it right into a telephone pole. Totaled it. I didn't get hurt, but now I have no car."

The third guy says, "Well, I got so drunk that when I got home, I cussed my girlfriend out and knocked over a candle, which lit the apartment on fire. She dumped me, all my belongings are destroyed, and the home insurance won't cover the damage."

The first guy motions the other two to come closer and whispers, "I'm not sure you understand. Chunks is my dog."

7

Our Systems Are Are Incompatible: Ethnic Jokes

N-WORD. K-WORD. And then there's "Polacks." Ethnic humor is the most American humor. In Europe you shoot first and laugh later. There aren't a lot of good ethnic jokes in Bosnia.

> Q: *What did the Croat say to the Serb?*
> A: *Bang. Bang.*

According to our studies—three days reading the newspaper on the toilet—there was an increase in "hate crimes" during the era when we attempted to cleanse ethnic humor. But thanks to the Great Anonymous Internet, we can be un-PC again and make fun of our roots. How sweet. We can be un-PC on our PCs.

Mamma mia! Alotta the ethnic humor floating around the Internet is the same old ethnic humor of a generation ago. Long after most people stopped thinking of themselves as Irish or Polish, we are still joking as if we do. This is America, where everyone fucks everyone else. We should have intermarried our way out of ethnic humor by now.

But why are there are so few jokes about the new immigrant groups? We should be picking on the new guys. Is it collective guilt over U.S. involvement in Latin America and Southeast Asia? (Hey, like guilt over slavery ever stopped racist humor.)

Is it because members of the establishment have moved so far from the urban centers that they don't even know what's funny about Russians? (Like WASPs ever buzzed around the inner city, anyway.)

We know—from, like, scientific research—the accuracy of the old, established stereotypes. But we don't know what a Guatemalan does. Or, is it simply that there is nothing funny about a Hmong?

> Q: *Did you see the schlong on that guy from Southeast Asia?*
>
> A: *It was hmongous.*

Ethnic humor depends on a sense of one's own identity. And with more and more of us becoming mestizos, what's to laugh at? Dobby is part Scottish, part German, part Norwegian, and part Zuni. Alice, on the other hand, is 100 percent pure kosher Jew. Yet this is America, where the two of us can get together and laugh at the Italians. It's all good-natured, though. Really, Don Corleone, we meant no disrespect when we called you "the Fairy Godfather."

So we must agree on a set of stereotypes that we will play against for what is called "ethnic" humor:

Stereotypes of the North American Peoples

1. Asian people can't drive. (They just make better cars.)
2. Jewish women are bitches (because Jewish men don't beat them).
3. Black men have huge penises. (So who needs affirmative action?)
4. Polish people are stupid. (Who else would live in Poland?)

5. Italians are all in the Mafia. (Wrong. A few are too stupid to join.)

6. Irish people are all drunks. (How else could they put up with the English?)

7. WASPs are as exciting as death. (That's why they like to kill everyone else.)

8. Mexicans eat beans. (This explains their slow integration into WASP society.)

9. Middle-Eastern women have mustaches. (We'd have a joke about Mohammed here, but we're afraid they'd kill us.)

10. Native Americans are drunks. (That's why everyone thinks they're Irish.)

Fear of the stranger is at the heart of ethnic humor. We've always made fun of the group in the next cave. As Cro-Magnon man said in the Paleolithic: "Did you hear the one about the Neanderthal who couldn't get laid?"

>> SUBJECT: Our Systems Are Incompatible (Ethnic Jokes)

>> A Scot, a Brit, and an Irishman walk into a bar. The bartender serves the brew in three mugs, one for each. In an amazing coincidence, three flies land in the heads of the brews, one for each.

The Brit wrinkles his face in disgust and pushes his mug away. The Scot nonchalantly plucks the fly out of his mug, flicks it away, and drinks. The Irishman picks up his fly, holds it up, and screams, "Spit it out, you bastard!"

>> Three Proofs That Jesus Was Jewish:

1. He went into his father's business.

2. He lived at home until the age of thirty-three.

3. He thought his mother was a virgin, and his mother thought he was God.

>> Three Proofs That Jesus Was Irish:

1. He never married.

2. He never held a steady job.

3. His last request was a drink.

>> Three Proofs That Jesus Was Christian:

1. He had no interest in sex.

2. He hosted the ultimate church potluck supper.

3. He liked to carry a cross.

>> Three Proofs That Jesus Was Puerto Rican:

1. His first name was Jesus.

2. He was always in trouble with the law.

3. His mother didn't know who his father was.

>> Three Proofs That Jesus Was Italian:

1. He talked with his hands.

2. He had wine with every meal.

3. He worked in the building trades.

>> Three Proofs That Jesus Was Black:

1. He called everybody brother.

2. He had no permanent address.

3. Nobody would hire him.

>> Three Proofs That Jesus Was Californian:

1. He never cut his hair.

2. He walked around barefoot.

3. He invented a new religion.

>> An old Indian walks into a bar, packing a dead cat in one hand and a bag of manure in the other and sporting a six-shooter in his belt. He puts the dead cat on the bar beside the bag of manure and tells the bartender, "Give me whiskey."

The Indian downs the whiskey, picks up the dead cat and takes a bite, then takes the pistol and shoots a hole in the bag of manure.

The bartender says, "Hey, chief, what the hell's going on?"

The Indian says, "Give me more whiskey."

The bartender pours some more, and the Indian slugs it down, picks up the dead cat and takes another bite, then takes the six-shooter and puts another round in the bag of manure.

The bartender says, "You crazy old fool, what the hell you trying to do?"

The Indian says, "Me want be like white man: drink whiskey, eat pussy, and shoot the shit."

>> Q: How do you know when your house has been robbed by an oriental gang member?

A: The dog is missing, and your homework is done.

>> An Irishman, a Mexican, and a redneck were doing construction work on a scaffolding on the twentieth floor of a building. They were eating lunch and the Irishman said, "Corned beef and cabbage! If I get corned beef and cabbage one more time for lunch I'm going to jump off this building."

The Mexican opened his lunch box and exclaimed, "Burritos again! If I get burritos one more time, I'm going to jump off, too."

The redneck opened his lunch and said, "Bologna again. If I get a bologna sandwich one more time, I'm jumping, too."

The next day, the Irishman opens his lunch box, sees corned beef and cabbage, and jumps to his death. The Mexican opens his lunch, sees a burrito, and jumps too. The redneck opens his lunch, sees the bologna, and jumps to his death also.

At the funeral, the Irishman's wife is weeping. She says, "If I'd known how really tired he was of corned beef and cabbage, I never would have given it to him again."

The Mexican's wife also weeps and says, "I could have given him tacos or enchiladas. I didn't realize he hated burritos so much."

Everyone turns and stares at the redneck's wife.

"Hey, don't look at me," she says. "He made his own damn lunch."

>> Sammy was up to his eyes in money troubles and could see no way out except winning the lottery. He went to the synagogue and prayed to win. At the next draw he waited confidently, but was disappointed. He returned to the synagogue and prayed again, pointing out that he had lived an exemplary religious life, devoutly observing rituals and dietary laws, contributing generously to Jewish charities, etc. Still at the next draw he didn't win. He returned to the synagogue close to despair, but before he could find the words a voice spoke to him out of the clouds: "OK, you want to win the lottery. But please, meet me halfway. Buy a ticket."

>> A young black couple are watching TV when their child speaks for the first time, saying "Mother."

With excitement, the father exclaims, "Did you hear that, baby? Our son just said half a word!"

>> After finishing dinner with a new girlfriend, a French fighter pilot retires to a couch where he immediately starts kissing her on the neck. After a few minutes of this the girlfriend says, "Kiss my lips." The French fighter pilot dips two fingers in some red wine, rubs it on her lips, and in a thick French accent says, "When I have red meat, I have red wine."

After kissing his girlfriend on her lips for a while she says, "Kiss me lower." The French fighter pilot then dips two fingers in some white wine, rubs them on her breasts, and says, "When I have white meat, I have white wine." Then he begins to kiss her breasts.

After a few minutes of this the girlfriend says in complete passion, "Kiss me lower!" The French fighter pilot then takes a bottle of cognac, pours it between her legs, and with a match he sets the cognac on fire. In disbelief the girlfriend jumps up and says, "What the hell are you doing?"

To which the French fighter pilot replies, "When I go down, I go down in flames."

>> A blonde was telling a priest a Polack joke, when halfway through the priest interrupts her. "Don't you know I'm Polish?"

"Oh, I'm sorry," the blonde apologizes. "Do you want me to start over and talk slower?"

>> Three boys, one black and two white, all third-graders, are playing after school. As boys tend to do, inevitably they start discussing who has the biggest one. To settle the matter, they agree to determine this once and for all by means of comparison. It turns out in favor of the black boy, who self-confidently boasts that he won, of course, because he's black.

He runs home to tell his mother: "Mom, Mom, guess what! We compared our pee-pees at the playground today, and I had the biggest one! That's because I'm black, right?"

"No, honey . . . that's because you're nineteen."

>> An American tourist goes into a restaurant in Spain and orders the specialty of the house. When his dinner arrives, he asks the waiter what it is.

"These, señor," replies the waiter, "are the—how you say?—the testicles of the bull killed in the ring today." The tourist is a bit squeamish, but tastes the dish and thinks it's delicious.

He comes back the next evening and orders the same thing. When it's served, he says to the waiter, "These cojónes are sure a lot smaller than the ones I had last night."

"Yes, señor," replied the waiter, "But you see, the bull, he does not always lose."

>> During World War II, a society lady who lived on Philadelphia's exclusive Main Line decided to be charitable and support the war effort by inviting three soldiers to Thanksgiving dinner. She called the nearby army base and was connected with a sergeant. He heard the lady's invitation and said he'd be glad to send three soldiers. Then the lady added, "Sergeant, I don't want any of them to be Jews."

"I understand, madame," said the sergeant.

So on Thanksgiving, there stood on the doorstep of the fine Main Line house three immaculately uniformed soldiers, all of them black. "We're here for Thanksgiving, madame," said one, politely.

The lady was astonished. "But, but . . ." she sputtered, "the sergeant must have made a mistake."

"Oh, no, madame," said the soldier, "Sergeant Cohen never makes a mistake."

» A white man noticed the impressive length of the black man's penis at the adjacent urinal.

"Sure wish I had one like yours."

The black man replied "You can. Just tie a string around it and hang a weight on the end of the string. Put the weight down your pant leg, and you can have one like mine."

The white man thanked him for the suggestion and left. Some weeks later, they met again in the lavatory. The black man asked how the project was going. "Great—I'm half way there."

"Really?" said the black man.

"Yes. It's black!"

» Three guys are in a bar: a Texan, a Californian, and a Seattleite. They drink, they get crazy.

The Texan grabs a bottle of tequila, unscrews the top, takes a good swig, and throws the bottle into the air. He then pulls out a forty-five-caliber pistol and shoots the bottle, spraying tequila all over everything.

The other patrons at the bar shout, "Hey why'd you waste that?"

The Texan says, "Hell, it's just tequila. Where I come from, we got lotsa tequila."

The Californian, not to be outdone, whips out a corkscrew and opens a bottle of Chardonnay, pours a bit into a glass, swirls it around, sips it, then throws the bottle in the air and shoots it with a little silver pistol.

The patrons again express their displeasure and astonishment at the waste of a bottle of good wine. The Californian says, "Napa Valley, we got lots of great wine up there."

The Seattleite borrows the corkscrew, pops the top off a bottle of Red Hook and downs the whole bottle. He throws the empty bottle into the air, shoots the Californian, and simultaneously catches the falling bottle.

Now the people are screaming, "Why'd you do that?"

The Seattleite replies, "I'm from Seattle. We got lots of Californians, but I got to recycle this bottle."

>> Jewish Pickup Lines

Hey, baby, wanna spin my dreidel?

Why is this night different from all other nights? You're about to find out.

I got fifty shares of Microsoft for my bar mitzvah. What'd you get for your bat mitzvah?

Wanna see my designer schlong? Mizrahi did my bris.

Is that a mezuzah in your pocket, or are you just happy to see me?

Can I part your Red Sea?

I've got a Ramses in my wallet that wants to put you back in slavery.

Nice tallis. Wanna fuck?

Why don't you slide your matzo balls over here next to my gefilte fish.

Some guys use whip cream. I'm a potato latke man myself.

>> An American tourist was driving outside of Rome when he decided to stop for a hitchhiker. To his surprise, the hitchhiker pulled a gun and, with a thick Italian accent, demanded that the tourist get out of the car.

"Don't kill me, please. Just take my money, take the car."

"I no-a kill you," the Italian replied, "as long as you do-a what I say. Now take-a out your dick and masturbate."

The shocked tourist did what he was told.

"Okay," said the Italian, "now do it again." The tourist wanted to protest, but the Italian had the gun pointed at him, so he did it one more time.

"Now one more-a time, or I-a kill you." With extreme effort the tourist brought himself to a third orgasm. Then the Italian gave a signal and a bellisima young woman stepped out from behind a big tree. "Now," said the Italian, "you can-a give my sister a ride to town."

>> A white girl just married to a black guy is nervous about the wedding night, as she's heard that black men are better endowed than white men.

She explains this to her husband, who tells her he knows how to get around the situation, which is to show her his penis bit by bit. First, he leaves the room.

The wife lies in bed and sees three inches of penis come round the door. "Are you nervous yet?" says her husband.

"No, I'm OK," she replies.

Another six inches of penis comes around the door, and he says, "Are you still OK?"

"Yes," she replies.

Another foot comes around the door, and she says "I'm still not nervous."

"OK," her husband replies. "I'm coming up the stairs."

>> Why did the Jew sell Christmas trees?

He was a pine Cohen.

>> What do Jews do on Christmas?

Dance around the cash register and sing, "What a friend we have in Jesus."

>> An immigrant from Czechoslovakia went to an optometrist for a checkup.

The doctor started with some simple testing, showing him a standard eye chart with the letters: CRKBNWXSKZY

The doc asked, "Can you read that?"

The Czech says, "Read it? Hell, Doc, I know him!"

>> Three hillbillies are ogling a pig.

First guy says, "I shore wish that was Marilyn Monroe."

Second guy says, "I shore wish it was Demi Moore."

Third guy says, "I shore wish it was dark already."

>> A man hated Italians. He complained to his friend, "They talk with their hands; they smell like garlic; they're always involved in some shady enterprise."

One day while walking down the street together, they saw an old Italian organ grinder standing on the corner, plying his trade. As they passed by, the man reached into his pocket, pulled out a twenty-dollar bill, and put it in the monkey's hat. The man's friend was surprised and said, "What are you doing? I thought you hated Italians!"

The man replied, "I do, but I feel sorry for their kids."

>> A Chinese couple is in bed one night, when the man gives his wife an elbow and says, "May-Ling, how about a little sixty-nine. I'm in the mood for some sixty-nine."

"Shut up and go back to sleep," groans his wife.

"Come on, you know I like sixty-nine, and you do too."

"What time is it?" she says.

"1:30 AM."

"If you think I'm gonna get up at this hour and make General Tsao's Chicken for you, you must be crazy.

God@
machina.ex

A NUN'S BREASTS, A PRIEST'S DRESS, a rabbi's habit—is nothing sacred? Not in the wonderful world of Internet jokes, where you can drag someone's religion into the gutter with just a drag of your mouse. It must be because computer people are godless that so many jokes on the wires degrade people of the cloth and even the Big Cloth Guy himself.

It's hard to find something funny about the Big Guy. Yes, He's a woman. Yes, He's mean. And there may be twelve of Him. As the old joke goes: If the cosmological equivalent of monotheism is the big bang, then the cosmological equivalent of polytheism is the gang bang.

What's funny about the different religions? Judging by the numbers of jokes, Catholics are the funniest. How did God make Catholics funny? Let us count the ways on our rosary beads:

1. Men in dresses
2. Bald women in dresses
3. Abstinence (altar boys don't count)
4. The wafer thing
5. The pay-as-you-go confession deal

In jokes, as in life, Jews come in second. The contrast between the secular Jew who loves money and the religious Jew who loves God is not always obvious to the observant goy. So, what's so funny about Jews, already?

1. The unkindest cut thing
2. The beanie
3. The babes in the balcony
4. Reformed rabbis
5. The sacred ceremony to make a thirteen year old rich

Protestants? You gotta love those guys. The poor ones are the wretched of the earth, and the rich ones are the WASPS who sting them. So where's the joke?

1. Speaking in tongues, handling snakes, believing the Bible, and committing adultery (Baptists)
2. Sexually active priests, centrally located cathedrals, and money (Episcopalians)
3. Tea sandwiches, dry Eucharist, and the Rotary Club (Presbyterians)
4. Funky God music, booty shaking, and free lunch (African Methodists)
5. No God, no Bible, family values, bad hair (generic Christians)

Many of the great world religions are excluded from the jokes we have culled. We would like to state unequivocally that the only reason there are no jokes about Islam here is because no one ever thought of one in the history of the world. Really. It's not that we're chicken. And Salman Rushdie is a lesbian, by the way.

There are no jokes here about Hindus because they're too busy programming. They're are no jokes about Sikhs and Jains because they're too busy watching their stock options.

Also notably absent is the great Buddhist religion, the favorite spiritual trip among the computer nerds formerly known as Jews. It's a popular form of worship we like to call Zen Judaism.

> *"What is the sound of one Jewish nerd praying?"*
> *"That, my son, is Zen Cohen."*

The above joke is so arcane that only about five people will get it. We have eliminated such in-jokes for the religiously literate in the following section, leaving us with mainly filth, blasphemy, and a little child molestation thrown in for the Catholics.

Apologies to the Goddess, who is missing in this action. She's too silly for humor.

>> SUBJECT: God@machina.ex

>> Old man Moskowitz was getting along in years. He decided to retire and let his three sons run the company (which manufactured a wide variety of nails). The sons thought they could increase market share with some judicious billboard advertising.

Only a week later, the old man was taking his usual Sunday drive in the country when he saw the first billboard ad. There it was—a picture of Christ on the cross, with the caption: "Nails for Every Purpose. Use Moskowitz Nails."

The old man immediately met with his three sons to voice his concern. "You can't show Christ on the cross, nailed there with our nails!" He explained that the backlash could be horrendous. The company could be ruined. The sons agreed that they would fix the ad campaign.

A week later the old man was again taking his usual Sunday drive when he saw the second billboard ad. There it was—a picture of the same cross, empty, with Christ crumpled on the ground below . . . and the caption: "Next Time Use Moskowitz Nails."

>> Two nuns are ordered to paint a room in the convent, and the last instruction of the mother superior is that they must not get even a drop of paint on their habits.

After conferring about this for a while, the two nuns decide to lock the door of the room, strip off their habits, and paint in the nude. In the middle of the project, there comes a knock at the door.

"Who is it?" calls one of the nuns.

"Blind man," replies a voice from the other side of the door.

The two nuns look at each other and shrug, and deciding that no harm can come from letting a blind man into the room, they open the door.

"Nice tits," says the man. "Where do you want these blinds?"

>> Jesus was searching the earth for his stepfather, but did not find him. Finally he sat down in Rome at the Vatican, beside an old man.

Old man: You look just like you have all the world's troubles on your shoulders, what's your problem?

Jesus: I am looking for my stepfather.

Old man: Funny, I have been looking for my stepson. What's the name of your stepfather?

Jesus: Joseph.

Old man: But that's my name, Giuseppe, in Italian. How do you otherwise recognize your stepfather?

Jesus: My stepfather was a carpenter.

Old man: But I am a carpenter. Any other ways to know your stepfather?

Jesus: When I was born, it was a miracle, and further I have holes in my hands and feet.

Old man: But that sounds exactly like my stepson.

Jesus [embracing the old man]: Father!

Old man [in tears]: Pinocchio!

>> A little boy is told by his mother that he has been very bad this year.

"What? Nothing for Christmas?" cried the little boy.

"Well," said Mom, "maybe if you write a letter to Baby Jesus and tell him how sorry you are, Santa will bring you some presents."

The little boy returned to his room and began his letter. With each attempt at writing, he would first apologize and then promise to be good for a certain amount of time. Eventually he crumpled up each letter, and started again, making the "be good"-time shorter with each effort. Finally, in frustration, he gave up, but then he was struck by a bolt of inspiration. Running to the living room, he carefully removed the little Mother Mary figure from the family's manger scene and carefully wrapped it in a sock, placing it in his top drawer. Returning to his desk, he took out a piece of paper and began to write:

"Dear Baby Jesus, if you ever want to see your mother again. . ."

>> Jesus and Moses are sitting around Heaven one day, bored. "Waddya wanna do today, Moses?" Jesus asks. "I don't know." Moses replies. "We've seen all the movies already. . . ." Eventually, they decide to go back and visit the earth.

While wandering across the surface of the globe, they come to the Red Sea. Moses stands on the shore, gazing across the waves. "You know," he says, "I'd like to see if I still have the old juice in me."

With these words, he stands tall, concentrates, and flings his arms toward the heavens. The clouds burst, the waters bubble, and then—in one huge, convulsive movement—the waves roll back and the sea parts.

Moses gazes with satisfaction at the path leading through the sea. "Yeah, nice to know I've still got what it takes." He lets his arms drop, and the waters crash back into place.

Later, the two men find themselves by the Sea of Galilee. "My turn now," Jesus says. "Let's see if I've still got my stuff. I haven't walked on water in years." So saying, he marches toward the shore.

He strides out right onto the surface of the water, turns around, and grins at Moses. Another few steps farther out, he sinks in just a little bit—perhaps as far as his ankles. A few more steps, and he sinks in up to his knees.

Gamely setting his face, he pushes forward another couple of steps, and then all buoyancy suddenly abandons him and he drops abruptly below the surface of the waves.

Jesus swims back to shore and hauls himself out of the water—a wet, bedraggled mess. Moses is rolling around on the sand, pointing and laughing, fit to bust a gut.

Jesus shakes his head sadly. "I just don't understand it. What could have gone wrong?"

"Schmuck!" Moses whoops. "You forgot about the holes in your feet!"

>> I was walking across a bridge one day, and I saw a man standing on the edge, about to jump off. So I ran over and said, "Stop! Don't do it!"

"Why shouldn't I?" he said.

I said, "Well, there's so much to live for."

He said, "Like what?"

I said, "Well . . . are you religious or atheist?"

He said, "Religious."

I said, "Me too. Are you Christian or Jewish?"

He said, "Christian."

I said, "Me too. Are you Catholic or Protestant?"

He said, "Protestant."

I said, "Me too. Are you Episcopalian or Baptist?"

He said, "Baptist."

I said, "Wow! Me too. Are you Baptist Church of God or Baptist Church of the Lord?"

He said, "Baptist Church of God."

I said, "Me too. Are you Original Baptist Church of God, or are you Reformed Baptist Church of God?"

He said, "Reformed Baptist Church of God."

I said, "Me too. Are you Reformed Baptist Church of God, reformation of 1879, or Reformed Baptist Church of God, reformation of 1915?"

He said, "Reformed Baptist Church of God, reformation of 1915."

I said, "Die, heretic scum," and pushed him off.

>> Jesus was having dinner with his disciples, and as they gathered reverentially about him, seated in the manner immortalized by Leonardo da Vinci, Jesus looked about at them.

There, on one side, he saw Judas Iscariot, who he knew would betray him before three hours had passed. On the other side was Peter, the prince of the disciples, whom he well knew would deny him thrice ere the cock crowed. And almost immediately opposite him was Thomas, who, on a crucial occasion, would express doubts.

There was only one thing to do.

Jesus called over the headwaiter. "Max," he said, "separate checks."

>> Guy goes to hell. As the Devil is in a good mood, on the first day, he shows the guy around so he can choose which damnation will fall on him.

The guy goes into the first room and sees people flogged by demons, with hundreds of flies feasting on their wounds. Horrified, he shuts the door and says, "I think I'll see a few more punishments, please."

He goes into a second room and sees people boiled alive in cauldrons, demons piercing their bodies with spears.

Despairing, he opens the third door. He sees Claudia Schiffer fucking some old guy while ten demons watch. Happy, he tells the devil, "OK, I want this punishment."

"OK," says the devil, and he calls the demons: "Guys, give this man the same punishment we gave Claudia Schiffer."

>> A bunch of preachers are having a meeting in the rectory of a Catholic priest. Just as they're silently tuning up for some heavy orations, the priest offers all of them a whiskey to ease tensions and get the smell of religious incense out of the air.

"Don't mind if I do, thanks," says the Methodist vicar, who slugs down three fingers of Wild Turkey.

"And you?" asks the priest of the born-again minister.

"What?" the minister shouts indignantly. "Drink alcohol? Why, I'd rather debauch in a whorehouse!"

At this the Methodist spits his whiskey back into the glass and hollers, "Whoa! You mean we get a choice?"

>> For decades, two heroic statues, one male and one female, faced each other in a city park. Then, one day, an angel came down from heaven.

"You've been such exemplary statues," he announced to them, "that I'm going to give you a special gift. I'm going to bring you both to life for thirty minutes, in which time you can do anything you want."

And with a clap of his hands, the angel brought the statues to life. The two approached each other a bit shyly, but soon dashed for the bushes, from which soon emerged a good deal of giggling, laughter, and shaking of branches.

Fifteen minutes later, the two statues emerged from the bushes, wide grins on their faces. "You still have fifteen more minutes," said the angel, winking at them.

Grinning even more widely, the female statue turned to the male statue and said, "Great! This time you hold the pigeon down, and I'll crap on its head."

>> A married woman is having an affair. Whenever her lover comes over, her nine-year-old son hides in the

closet and watches them. One day the woman hears a car pull into the driveway and tells her lover to hide in the closet, as she fears he will not be able to sneak out fast enough. Inside the closet, the little boy says, "It's dark in here, isn't it?"

"Yes it is," the man replies nervously, realizing that they've been observed in a very compromising situation.

"Ya wanna buy a baseball?' the little boy asks.

"No thanks," the man replies.

And the kid says, "I think you do wanna buy a baseball.

"OK, how much?" the man replies after considering the position he's in.

"Twenty-five dollars," the little extortionist replies.

"Twenty-five dollars?" the man repeats incredulously, but coughs up the bucks to keep the kid quiet.

The following week, the lover is visiting the woman again, when she hears a car in the driveway and again, asks him to hide in the closet.

"Dark in here, isn't it?" the boy starts off.

"Yes it is," whispers the man.

"Wanna buy a baseball glove," the kid asks.

"OK, how much?" asks the clandestine lover.

"Fifty dollars," the boy replies, and the deal is done.

The next weekend, the little boy's father says, "Hey sonny, go get your new ball and glove, and we'll play some catch."

"Can't do it, Daddy," the boy says. "I sold them."

"What? You sold them? How much did you get?"

"I got seventy-five dollars," the little boy bragged.

"Seventy-five dollars! You little thief. OK. I'm taking you to the church right now. You must confess your sin and ask for forgiveness." And he hauls the little boy away.

At the church, the little boy goes into the confessional, draws the curtain, sits down, and says, "Boy, it's dark in here, isn't it?"

"Don't you start that shit in here now," responds the priest.

>> The pope went on a tour of America. When his plane landed, a large crowd was at the airport to meet him. As he stepped out of the plane, the crowd called out "Elvis! Elvis, we love you! We love you, Elvis!"

The pope wondered what was going on. He tried to say "I'm-a not-a Elvis," but no one could hear him over the noise of the crowd.

While he was being driven to his hotel, the streets were lined with cheering people. "Elvis! Elvis, we love you! We love you Elvis!

"But I'm-a not-a Elvis," the pope insisted. Still, no one heard.

The pope was then taken to his hotel room. He stepped inside and shut the door. He turned around to see a scantily clad, beautiful young woman on the bed. "Elvis," she moaned. "Elvis, take me. Do what you will with me. I love you, Elvis."

The Pope started to sing, "Well-a bless-a my soul, what's-a wrong with me . . ."

>> A priest and a rabbi were talking when the rabbi asked the priest about confession. "I have an idea," said the priest. "Why don't you sit with me on my side of the confession booth and hear it for yourself? No one will ever know."

A woman came into the booth and said, "Bless me, Father, for I have sinned."

The priest asked, "What did you do?"

"I cheated on my husband."

"How many times?"

"Three times."

"Well," said the priest, "say five Hail Marys and put five dollars in the offering box."

Another woman came and said, "Bless me, Father, for I have sinned."

The priest asked, "What did you do?"

"I cheated on my husband."

"How many times?"

"Three times."

Again the priest said, "Say five Hail Marys and put five dollars in the offering box."

Then the priest said to the rabbi, "Would you like to do the next confession?" The rabbi started to object, but the priest said, "Go ahead. It's easy."

So another woman came in and said, "Bless me, Father, for I have sinned."

This time the rabbi asked, "What did you do?"

"I cheated on my husband."

"How many times?"

The woman said, "Twice."

Then the rabbi said, "Well, go do it again. They're three for five dollars today."

>> It's a dreary Saturday afternoon at the local church, and a priest is sitting in the confessional. All of a sudden, he has to go to the bathroom. He asks the altar boy to mind the confessional until he returns.

After the priest leaves, a woman enters the other side and begins to confess a sexual encounter she had the previous evening: "Father, forgive me, for I have sinned. I gave oral sex to a man in his car last night. I am sorry and ready to repent. What do I get for giving this man oral pleasure?"

To which the altar boy replies, "Well, Father Smith usually gives us a Snickers and a Coke."

>> A priest was walking down the street, and a ho came up to him and said, "Hey, guy! How would you like a little head?"

Confused, he asked, "What's a little head?"

She laughed her ass off, and he just kept on walking. When he got back to the church, he asked one of the nuns, "What's a little head?"

She said, "Twenty dollars, just like in town."

>> This homely old nun was walking home from the convent one day, when this man jumps out from the bushes and has his way with her. Then the man says, "What will you tell the Holy Father now, Sister?"

She says, "I must tell the truth! I will say I was walking home from the convent when a man jumped out from the bushes and raped me twice—unless you're too tired."

>> One day a nun was fishing and caught a huge fish for supper. A man was walking by and said, "Wow! What a goddamn fish!"

The sister said, "Sir, you shouldn't talk to me like that. I'm a nun."

The man said, "But that's the name of it, a 'goddamn fish.'"

The sister took the fish back to the rectory and said, "Mother Superior, look at the goddamn fish I caught."

The mother superior said, "Sister, you shouldn't talk like that!"

The sister said, "But Mother Superior, that's the name of it, a 'goddamn fish.'"

So the mother superior said, "Well, give me the goddamn fish, and I'll clean it."

While she was cleaning the fish the monsignor walked in and she said, "Monsignor, look at the goddamn fish that the sister caught."

The monsignor said, "Mother Superior, you shouldn't talk like that!" The mother superior said, "But that's the name of it, a 'goddamn fish.'"

The monsignor said, "Well give me the goddamn fish, and I'll cook it."

That evening at supper there was a new priest at the table, and he said, "Wow, what a nice fish." And the sister said, "I caught the goddamn fish." And mother superior said, "I cleaned the goddamn fish." And the monsignor said, "I cooked the goddamn fish."

And the new priest said, "I like this fucking place already!"

>> A fellow was visiting the Vatican and became separated from his tour group. After wandering for a while, he needed to relieve himself. He finally found a bathroom and wandered in. You can imagine his surprise to discover the pope sitting on the toilet, masturbating. Figuring that this would be an attraction few tourists ever saw, he snapped a couple of pictures. The pope managed to recover his composure and offered the fellow $10,000 for the camera. The fellow decide to take him up on the offer and an exchange was arranged.

The camera was a pretty nice unit, so after disposing of the film, the pope decided he would use it on his world travels. One day while visiting a foreign country, one of the faithful noticed the pope's camera and remarked that it was quite a unit. He then asked, "How much did you pay for it?"

"Ten thousand dollars."

"Wow! The guy who sold you that must have seen you coming."

Guy Goes to a Doctor (or a Nurse-Practitioner)

IS THERE ANY SITUATION more pregnant with humor than the one in which you walk in a room, strip naked before a perfect stranger, and begin to discuss your pain as he places his face close to your throat, vagina, anus, or big toe? But enough about prostitution, we're talkin' doctors.

Alice, as a nurse-practitioner, has been performing rectal and pelvic exams for years. She knows that in these situations it is much more blessed to give than to receive.

In professional situations, the actual viewing of the pained body is often preceded by the patient's recitation of a long list of apologies for a bod gone bad. People like to warn, "I haven't bathed, brushed my teeth, wiped my ass...," but the health professional pushes on.

The worst patient was the young man who apologized for his tattoo. Alice, unmoved said, "Oh, trust me, I've seen it all." Yet she was not able to stifle a tiny gasp when the seven-inch letters spelling out "FUCK YOU" appeared across both pecs.

So you have the Guy-Goes-to-a-Doctor joke, an inherently funny situation, with its ability to invoke sympathetic fear and embarrassment in the reader. Add to this the great progress in modern medicine that is generally expressed in jokes as, "We have good news and we have bad news."

> Woman: Doctor can you really cure my cancer?
> Doctor: Well there's good news and there's bad.
> Woman: Gimme the good news first.

Doctor: We can cure your cancer.

Woman: And the bad?

Doctor: We'll have to change you into a laboratory animal first.

You might think from the jokes that follow that nobody goes to a doctor for anything other than a rectal exam. But that's the extreme case. It can be just as humiliating to have a doctor look in your ear. Especially if he starts saying things like, "Wow. Oh, my god! There's a tiny little nativity scene in here. . . . "

Add to embarrassment, nudity, and good and bad news, the economic chaos of recent medicine. (Thanks to our government for democratizing health care. We haven't insured more people, but the middle class now gets treated like shit too.)

What innovations have health maintenance organizations inflicted on us?

1. They save the insurance companies money (over your dead body).

2. You don't have to stay in the hospital (even after a brain surgery).

3. If you want to spend an extra night after a mastectomy, they'll throw in the other breast free.

4. You get to choose your personal physician from a list of recent graduates of Albania Tech. (The other doctors are taken.)

5. Natural childbirth and brief post-partum hospital stays. (Translation: Bite this strap, drink this whiskey, drop it, and you and the brat get the hell out of here.)

The situation in the Guy-Goes-to-a-Doctor joke is further complicated by the inherently unequal relationship between the two people. It makes marriage look fair. You almost want to say, "Physician, go fuck thyself."

(Hey kids, here's a little tip. Next time you go to the doctor, wear a white coat and ask her to take her clothes off.)

Further deification is conferred on the doctor by her title. She is Doctor Schmuck, while you are merely Dobby Schmuck. "Hey, schmuck, Doctor Schmuck will see you now."

Many people even prefer the torture of the dentist to the humiliation of the doctor, because they can keep their clothes on, and they can also request laughing gas. Think of how much fun a pelvic or a rectal would be with a little nitrous. "Oh, Doc, this is so groovy. Shove that cold metal instrument in a little harder!"

A common theme in doctor jokes is the absurdity of the treatments. People think the doctor's diagnosis may be accurate, but the treatment is ridiculous.

> Doctor: Go home and ice it and elevate it above the level of your heart.
>
> Patient: For a urinary tract infection?

Perhaps the problem is that most people feel the only good thing doctors have is antibiotics, and the rest is just witch doctor bullshit. This, of course, is why doctors always tell you the one thing you don't need is antibiotics.

But hey, we love doctors. In the unfortunate event that either of us ever needs brain surgery, you know, guys, just kidding here. Please, don't take the right lobe, OK?

>> SUBJECT: Guy Goes to a Doctor (or a Nurse-Practitioner)

>> A woman accompanied her husband to the doctor's office. After the checkup the doctor took the wife aside and said, "Your husband is suffering from severe long-term stress, and it's affecting his cardiovascular system. He's a good candidate for either a heart attack or a stroke. If you don't do the following four things, your husband will surely die."

"First, each morning, wake up and make love to him. Then, fix him a healthy breakfast and send him off to work in a good mood."

"Second, at lunch time, make him a warm, nutritious meal and give him a little hand job to put him in a good frame of mind before he goes back to work."

"Third, for dinner, fix an especially nice meal, and don't burden him with household chores."

"Fourth, and most important for invigorating him and relieving stress, have sex with him several times after dinner. Be sure to satisfy his every whim in bed. And don't forget the blow job just before he nods off."

On the way home in the car, the husband turned to his wife and asked, "So, I saw the doctor talking to you, and he sure seemed serious. What did he tell you?"

"You're going to die," she replied.

>> A retired man was having a unique problem. He discovered that his penis was turning orange. He was baffled, so he went to the local doctor's office to show him his problem. The doctor says to him, "I'm dumbfounded how someone's penis can all of a sudden turn orange. Are you out in the sun very often?"

The retired man said, "All I do all day is sit at home and watch porn films and eat Cheetos."

>> Guy goes to the doctor and is told he has only six hours to live. He rushes home and tells his wife and then says, "Let's make love." They do and then they fall asleep. A couple of hours later he wakes up and says, "Honey, let's do it again." They do and again after a very brief nap he says to her, "Honey, how about doing it one more time?"

She replies, "Aw, come on, I have to get up in the morning. You don't."

>> Guy walks into the doctor's office and requests a consultation. The nurse shows him to a room and asks him to strip down and await the doctor's arrival. The man removes his shirt and waits.

The doctor greets the patient and asks what the problem seems to be.

The man says, "W-w-well, y-you see th-that I-I have this sp-speech impediment, and the w-w-wife and I have d-discussed the problem and w-would like you to l-look into the matter."

The doctor says, "Didn't the nurse ask you to strip completely so I can examine you properly? Please do so."

Whereupon, the man strips, revealing the most enormous organ dangling between his legs, and the doctor says immediately, "I know exactly what your problem is. You see, your penis is so large and heavy that it is producing tremendous strain on your vocal cords all the way down to your groin. That's why you are having this stammering condition."

The man pleads, "Oh Doctor! Th-this is so fr-frustrating and emb-bara-ssing, I w-wish you c-could d-do something!"

The good doctor says, "Have no fear. With your permission and with the marvels of modern technology and medicine at our disposal these days, we can perform some minor corrective surgery (a la Bobbitt) and fit you with a more normal penis. After that (and a bit of speech therapy), you'll speak quite normally."

The man says gratefully, "Oh! P-p-lease do! Th-thank you."

Following the surgery, the hospital staff gives the man some instructions and asks him to return for a checkup within ninety days.

About forty-five days later, the man returns to the clinic and requests to see the doctor right away. The nurse asks him to be patient, but upon his insistence, shows him to the examining room to await the doctor's arrival.

As soon as the door opens and the doctor comes in, the man blurts out, "Oh, doctor! Thank God you're still here! Listen, the wife and I have been discussing the situation after my recent surgery, and while we are very pleased with your ridding me of my speech impediment—I mean, you can see how I can speak so fluently and clearly now, but we are quite dissatisfied with our sex life compared to before and implore you to restore me to my original genital state."

The good doctor regards his patient ruefully and replies, "S-s-sorry. A d-d-deal is a d-d-deal."

>> A man goes to a sperm bank to make a donation. To his surprise, he is ushered into an attractive room with a waterbed and soft music. A gorgeous naked woman arrives and hands him a fur-lined goblet. She dances seductively while he emits his specimen into the cup. Feeling refreshed, he goes to check out at the desk. He discovers several men standing in the hall ejaculating into paper cups.

"I don't understand," he says. "I had the nice room, the beautiful woman, the fur-lined goblet."

"Oh," says the receptionist, "they've got Kaiser[1]."

>> A guy with a long history of migraine headaches goes to the doctor. When the doctor does his history and physical, he discovers that his poor patient has had practically every therapy known to man for his migraines and still has shown no improvement.

"Listen," says the doc, "I have migraines too, and the advice I'm going to give you isn't really anything I learned in medical school, but it's advice that I've gotten from my own experience. When I have a migraine, I go home, get in a nice hot bathtub, and soak for a while. Then I have my wife sponge me off with the hottest water I can stand, especially

---

1. A notorious California-based HMO

around the forehead. This helps a little. Then I get out of the tub, take her into the bedroom, and even if my head is killing me, I force myself to have sex with her. Almost always, the headache is immediately gone. Now, give it a try, and come back and see me in six weeks."

Six weeks later, the patient returns with a big grin. "Doc! I took your advice and it works! It really works! I've had migraines for seventeen years, and this is the first time anyone has ever helped me."

"Well," says the physician, "I'm glad I could help."

"By the way, Doc," the patient adds, "you have a really nice house."

>> Three guys died at the same time and ended up in front of Peter at the pearly gates.

St. Peter says to the first guy, "Why should I let you in?" The guy answers, "Well, I was a doctor, and I helped many people get well." St. Peter says, "OK, you may come in."

St. Peter says to the second guy, "Why should I let you in?" This guy says, "I was a lawyer, and I defended many innocent people." St. Peter says, "OK, you may come in."

St. Peter says to the last guy, "And why should I let you in?" The guy answers, "Well, I was a managed care professional, and I helped to keep health-care costs down."

St. Peter thought about this a moment. Then he said, "OK, you may come in. But you can only stay three days."

>> A man suffering from a severe case of flatulence goes to the doctor.

Man: Doctor, I have a terrible (FARRRT!) problem. I just can't (FFFART!) stop farting.

Doctor: That is an unusual complaint. Take off your clothes and lie, stomach down, on the couch. (The man does as he is told. The doctor examines him for a minute, the man farting all the time this is going on.)

Doctor: Aha! This should be easy to cure. Excuse me for a moment. (The doctor goes over to a closet and pulls out an enormous long pole with a huge sharp spike at one end.)

Man: (FAART!) Oh my God! (FARRRT!) What are you going to do with (FFFARTT!!) that?!

Doctor: I need to open a window.

>> Guy goes to a doctor for an exam. The nurse asks him for a urine sample, a stool sample, a blood sample, and a semen sample, so he just gives her his underpants.

>> Doctor [taking up his stethoscope]: Big breaths.

Adolescent Blonde: Yeth, and I'm not even thixteen.

>> A gay guy comes into the doctor's office, and says, "Something's up my ass."

The doctor looks at him, puts on the rubber glove, and up the ass he goes. The guy is moaning, but the doctor keeps probing. "Nothing there," the doctor says.

"Go deeper," the guy says.

"Still nothing there," the doctor tells the guy.

"Deeper. Even deeper."

The doctor says, "Nothing there, man. Oh wait, there is. What the hell?!" He pulls out a dozen long-stemmed roses and shows them to the guy.

The guy smiles and asks, "Is there a card?"

>> A nurse is giving a sponge bath to a woman in a coma, when she notices that, when she washes the patient's "private area," there is a response on the monitor. The nurse contacts the patient's husband and explains what happened, telling him, "Crazy as this sounds, maybe a little oral sex will do the trick and bring her out of the coma." The husband is skeptical, but they assure him that they'll close the curtains for privacy. Besides, it's worth a try; there's nothing to lose.

The husband finally agrees and goes into his wife's room. After a few minutes the woman's monitor flatlines—no pulse, no heart rate.

The nurses run into the room. The husband is standing there, pulling up his pants, and says, "I think she choked."

>> A man, feeling poorly, goes to his doctor for an examination. The doc performs lots of tests, takes blood and urine samples, etc. He sends the man home and tells him to come back next week. At the next appointment, the man says, "So Doc, what's wrong with me?"

"Well, I'm afraid it's not good: you've got HES."

"HES? What's that?"

"Hepatitis, E. coli, and syphilis."

"Oh no! What am I going to do?"

"Well, first thing we've got to do is get you checked into a hospital. After that, we'll put you on a diet of pancakes, pizza, and fried flounder."

"What's so special about those foods?"

"They're the only things that will fit under the door."

>> A doctor goes to the same bar every day and orders the same drink, day in, day out. "Fix me an almond daiquiri, Dick," he always asks.

"Coming right up," says the bartender. And it goes on this way for years.

Finally one day, the bartender realizes that there are no more almonds anywhere in his inventory, and his customer is waiting anxiously at the bar for his favorite beverage. In a hurry, the bartender figures that he can use a hickory nut, crush it up, and the man will never know the difference. Well, the doctor takes a sip of the drink and says, "Is this an almond daiquiri, Dick."

"Well, no, it's a hickory daiquiri, Doc."

>> A couple, age seventy, went to the doctor's office. The doctor asked, "What can I do for you?"

The man said, "Will you watch us have sexual intercourse?"

The doctor looked puzzled but agreed. When the couple had finished, the doctor said, "There is nothing wrong with the way you have intercourse," and charged them thirty dollars. This happened several weeks in a row. The couple would make an appointment, have intercourse, pay the doctor, and leave. Finally the doctor asked, "Just exactly what are you trying to find out?"

The old man said, "We're not trying to find out anything. She's married, so we can't go to her house. I'm married, so we can't go to my house. The Holiday Inn charges fifty-five dollars, the Hilton charges eighty dollars, we do it here for thirty dollars and I get back twenty-six dollars from Medicare for a visit to the doctor's office."

>> A couple had been married for fifteen years and had always enjoyed a healthy sex life and a joyous relationship together. One night while getting it on, the man said to his wife, "You know, after having three kids, your twat isn't as tight as it used to be." He said it in his normal courteous tone, and the statement did not hurt her feelings. Instead, wishing to please her man, she decided to try to do something about it.

She went to the doctor, and he said that other than painful stitches, a regimen of targeted exercises would be the only thing that he could suggest to tighten her vagina. She opted for the exercises, and he gave her a computer printout with detailed instructions.

She got home that evening and began reading the exercise instructions: (1) Disrobe. (2) Place a mirror on the floor. (3) Squat over the mirror and look at the reflection of your bottom.

Her husband walked in just before she got to step four. She was only moderately embarrassed, and he was a little surprised. He said, "Hi honey, what are you doing there?"

She replied, "Oh, this. Well, I went to the doctor, and he gave me some exercises to help me tighten my pussy."

The husband said, "Oh, OK. Well, I'll leave so you can do them. Just watch out and don't fall in that big hole in the floor."

>> A fella complained to his friend, "My elbow really hurts. I guess I should see a doctor." His friend offered, "Don't do that. There's a computer in the lobby of the local hospital that can diagnose anything quicker and cheaper and more accurately than even their own doctors or nurse-practitioners. Simply put in a sample of your urine, and the computer will diagnose your problem and tell you what you can do about it. And it only costs ten dollars"

Figuring he had nothing to lose, the fella filled a jar with urine and went to the local hospital. Finding the computer, he poured in the sample and deposited the ten dollars. The computer started making some noises and various lights started to flash. After a brief pause, a small piece of paper popped out, on which was printed: "You have tennis elbow. Soak your arm in warm water, avoid heavy labor, and it will be better in two weeks." Later that evening, while thinking how amazing this new technology was and how it could change medical science forever, he began to wonder if the computer could be fooled.

He decided to give it a try. He mixed together some tap water, a stool sample from his dog, urine samples from his wife and daughter, and—to top it off—he masturbated into the concoction. He went back to the hospital and poured the sample in while depositing his ten dollars. The computer began making the usual noise and printed out the following analysis:

"Your tap water is hard. Get a softener."

"Your dog has worms. Give him vitamins."

"Your daughter's on drugs. Put her in rehab."

"Your wife's pregnant. It ain't yours. Get a lawyer."

"If you don't stop jerking off like that, your 'tennis elbow' will never get better."

>> There was a ninety-eight-year-old man who moved into a nursing home. For his age, he was very fit and in good shape. The doctor came in to give him his physical, and the man said, "How old do you think I am?"

The doctor checked his heart and lungs and had him do a few exercises and said, "I would say you were around seventy-eight." The old man smiled and the doctor was amazed that this man was indeed ninety-eight years old.

The man was walking out of the doctor's office and saw a little old lady sitting there. She was gray-haired and all bent over. The man said to the lady, "How old do you think I am?" She looked him over pretty good then told him to pull down his pants. He did as he was told. Then she told him to pull his underwear down also. He obeyed. She reached over and fondled his various parts and counterparts. She kept this up for quite some time. She appeared to be in deep concentration.

She finally looked up at the man and said, "I'd say you were ninety-eight."

The man was stunned. He said, "How could you tell?"

She said, "I heard you tell the doctor."

>> A ninety-year-old man goes to a doctor, sobbing. The doctor asks him what's wrong. Through his tears the old man answers, "I'm in love with a twenty-five-year-old woman."

"What's wrong with that?" asks the doctor.

Between his sobs and sniffles, the man answers, "You don't understand. Every morning before she goes to work, we make love. At lunch time she comes home, and we make love again, and then she makes my favorite meal. In the afternoon when she gets a break, she rushes home and gives me oral sex, the best an old man could want. And then, at supper time, and all night long, we make love." He breaks down, no longer able to speak.

The doctor puts his arm around the old man. "I don't understand. It sounds like you have the perfect relationship. Why are you crying?"

The old man bawls through his tears, "I forgot where I live!"

10

Musicians
Do It with
Horns

MUSICIANS ARE SPACE CASES. They spend too much time in nonverbal space or spacing out on drugs, booze, or the muse. There's something funny about someone who's "with it" and not all there.

As the old joke goes: Stop a musician on the street and ask him how to get to Carnegie Hall, and he'll say, "Practice." He's not thinking about reality, he's thinking about music. He's whistling. He's somewhere over the rainbow. He's out of it. It's fun to make jokes about musicians, just as it's fun to make jokes about morons.

> Guy: Hey, piano player, do you know the one about the mermaid who was a nice piece of tail?
>
> Musician: Hum a few bars and I'll fake it.

Part of the charm of the musician is his distractedness, which borders on innocence. For some reason drummers are thought to be the most innocent (i.e. stupid). But every musician is "gone" in his own way.

What They're Thinking While Playing "My Funny Valentine"

Pianist: Go ahead put a bill in the glass, asshole.

Trumpeter: Now I can cut one and nobody'll notice.

Saxophone player: Gee, I like blowing on this mouth piece.

Bass Player: Man, I gotta pee.

Chick Singer: They love me. They love me. Everyone loves me.

Audience: I wonder if the chick singer is fucking the drummer?

Drummer: Duh. Duh, Duh. Duh. Duh-Duh.

Because musicians have rhythm, we think they've also got great sex lives. Musicians are sex symbols by nature of their distractedness. It's as if they're on the verge of orgasm all the time. They moan in public. They scream out, "Yeah!"

Drugs, while part of the tragedy of the musical world, also contribute to what's funny about musicians. Drugs make you stupider, and they make you feel smarter. Drugs make you more distracted. Drugs make you more wondrous. In short, drugs make you a musician. We intend no endorsement of drugs here. Why would we want anyone to get wasted, stoned, or fucked up by smoking some shit or doing some weed?

But not all drugs are good for you. Crack kills. Heroin kills the pain and the brain. And speed makes you act like an American. Prozac is prosaic. Valium invalidates. And ecstasy is wasted on the young.

Funny, we started talking about musicians and now we're talking about drugs. Like love and marriage, ya can't have one without the other. Imagine Frank Sinatra without a drink, Jerry Garcia without a joint, or John Tesh without a cup of Ovaltine.

It's easy to make fun of bad musicians. Everybody likes to pick on Kenny G. But if you think he's bad, you should've heard Kenny A, B, C, D, E, and F. (F was the worst, man.)

Jokes have their rhythm, their own music. It's all in the ti-ti-ti-timing. That's why a little drum riff sounds after the punch line.

> Q. *What do you call a musician who just broke up with his girlfriend?*
>
> A. *Homeless.*

Ka-boom. The end.

>> SUBJECT: Musicians Do It with Horns

>> A violinist was returning home from a two-week trip. As he drove up to his house, he saw that it had burned to the ground. A fireman stood over the smoking rubble.

"What happened?" said the violinist.

"Well sir," the fireman said sadly, "your conductor came to your house this morning, raped and killed your wife and daughter, and burned down your house."

The violinist staggered. "The conductor came to see me?!"

>> This trumpet player dies. He gets to the pearly gates and tells St. Peter his name. St. Peter looks over "the list," raising an eyebrow or muttering occasionally. Finally he spots the name and says, "Oh, yes. We've been waiting for you."

"You have?"

"Oh, yes, indeed."

"So what's up, man?"

"Well, I have some good news and some bad news for you. Which would you like first?"

"Uh, well, how about the good news?"

"The good news is that we need a lead trumpet for our house band."

"That's cool. Tell me more."

"Well, the rest of the trumpet section is Miles and Satchmo and Chet and several more in rotation."

"Too much! Go on!"

"And the saxophone section is, as you can imagine, rather crowded, 'Trane and Bird and Ben and Prez and all the great cats."

"Wow."

"The rhythm section. . . must I read all these names? Suffice it to say that you will be in good company."

"And this is for eternity?"

"Yes."

"That's like *forever*, man?"

"Of course?"

"This is too cool. And you want *me* to play lead?"

"Yes."

"No shit. So what's the bad news? I mean, *nothing* could be bad compared to all this."

"The bad news is, God has this chick singer. . . ."

>> These two cowboys are riding out West and in the distance they hear the ominous sound of drums.

"Boy, I sure don't like the sound of those drums."

"Yeah, me neither. But it's not their regular drummer."

>> Q. What's the difference between a savings bond and a musician?

A: One will eventually mature and make some money.

>> Q: How many singers does it take to sing "My Funny Valentine"?

A: Apparently all of them.

>> Q: What do you call a guy who hangs out with musicians?

A: A drummer.

>> Q: What do the Somalians and Yoko Ono have in common?

A: They both live off dead Beatles.

>> Q: What do you get when you play New Age music backward?

A: New Age music.

>> Q: How do you know when the lead vocalist is at the door?

A: She can't find the key and doesn't know when to come in.

>> Q: What do you get when you play country music backward?

A: You stop drinking and get your job back and get your wife back.

>> Q: What has forty-two teeth and eighty-nine legs?

A: The front row of a Willie Nelson concert.

>> Q: What did the drummer get on his IQ test?

A: Drool.

>> Q: What's the difference between an AK-47 and Kenny G?

A: An AK-47 only repeats itself 100 times a minute.

>> Q: How many bass players does it take to change a lightbulb?

A: Only one, but the guitarist has to show them how do to do it first.

>> Q: How many bass players does it take to change a lightbulb?

A: None. The piano player does it with his left hand.

>> Q: How many bass players does it take to change a lightbulb?

A: Doesn't matter; nobody will notice anyway.

>> Q: How can you tell when a drummer is knocking at your door?

A: He rushes.

>> Q: What's the difference between a bull and an orchestra.

A: The bull has horns in the front and an asshole in back.

>> Q: Why did God make drummers ten IQ points smarter than horses?

A: So they wouldn't shit in the street during parades.

>> Q: What do you call a rock-and-roll musician who knows four chords?

A: Talented.

>> Q: What's brown and sits on a piano?

A: Beethoven's last movement.

>> A piano player goes to a nightclub owner and asks for a gig. The owner says, "Play me something." So the piano player sits down and plays the most hauntingly beautiful ballad. The few people in the club stop what they are doing and listen, entranced. At

the end there is silence, then spontaneous applause. The owner asks the piano player what that tune was.

The piano player says, "Oh, I wrote that. It's called 'You're a Cunt, You're a Bitch, Fuck You.'"

The owner shakes his head, then asks the piano player to play something up-tempo. The piano player plays a swinging, rocking tune that has the people snapping their fingers, smiling, wanting to dance. At the end, the club owner asks him what that tune was.

The piano player answers, "I call that one 'Stick it Up Your Ass, Motherfucker.'"

The club owner shakes his head, but says, "OK, man. You can play tonight. But don't announce the tunes. Just play, don't say anything."

That night the piano player sits down for his first set and plays great. After the first tune, the applause is so loud and long, the piano player stands up to take a bow. As he does so, a guy in the first row calls out, "Hey man, do you know your fly is open and your dick is hanging out?"

As he bows, the piano player replies, "Know it? I wrote it."

>> A man walks into a store. Humming tunelessly to himself, he saunters up to the counter where a clerk is busily involved with some apparently scintillating paperwork. The man somewhat shyly clears his throat and, in a hesitant voice, asks, "Excuse me, I'd like to try out one of those, um, Gibson Flatoblasters, and, uh, a Marshall amplificator, and, um, uh, one of those digital relay lines."

The clerk does not stop his work. In fact, he doesn't even look up. In a flat even tone, he replies, "You're a drummer, aren't you?"

Flattered to be so recognized, the man immediately brightens and replies cheerfully, "Yes, how did you know?"

The clerk, still so absorbed in his paperwork that he can't be troubled to look up, informs the man, "Well, for a start, this is a travel agency."

>> At a classy restaurant where only a select crowd gets in, the maitre d' interrogates the would-be customers.

Maitre d': So how much do you make?

Customer one: $100,000 a year.

Maitre d': What do you do?

Customer one: I'm a lawyer.

Maitre d': Come right in.

Maitre d'[to Customer two]: How much do you make?

Customer two: $10,000 a year.

Maitre d': So what instrument do you play?

>> An anthropologist goes to Africa to study a tribe deep in the jungle. All through the first day he hears constant drumming in the jungle and he wonders if there is any ominous meaning to it, but the locals don't seem concerned, so he doesn't mention it. The drumming continues on the second and third

days, and he still wonders what's up, but no one else seems worried so he doesn't ask.

On the fourth day, the drumming stops and the anthropologist notices the chief has a worried look on his face. So he asks if something's wrong.

The chief says, "Drumming stopped. Very bad."

The anthropologist asks what's going to happen next. The chief, looking very concerned, replies, "Bass solo."

Academia: The Ivory Dildo

YOU WOULD THINK with how little they have to do and all that free Internet time that there'd be a bumper crop of jokes by academics, for academics, about what schmucks academics are. Instead they spend their time bookmarking erotica on the web and e-mailing jokes. As one academic friend e-mailed recently along with an attachment of really ba-a-a-d jokes: "As a college professor, this is the most constructive thing I can do."

He wasn't kidding.

Academics have always been famous for their lack of a sense of humor about themselves.

> Q: Did you hear the one about the English professor and the math professor?
>
> A. One counts rhymes; the other is a stunning cunt.

But seriously folks, the only way academics will deal with their ridiculousness is to write books satirizing academia. Nobody reads these books but other academics because their books, like their jokes, are too long (much like a fifty-minute classroom lecture or Polonius's too long "Brevity is the soul of wit" speech).

We had to spend hours editing academic jokes here. We've become the Lorena Bobbitts of academic humor. Some of the original jokes were over three hundred-pages long. Maybe they worked as theses.

There has to be something funny about people who make $100,000 for working twenty minutes a week (not including the six months' vacation time and the three-year sabbaticals every two years). As the old joke goes, a professor is someone who believes he deserves a sinecure because he knows the meaning of the word.

Dobby, a college teacher, likes to remind his students of the central difference between him as teacher and them as students: He is being paid to be there, and they are paying to be there. He has the better deal.

Yet most the jokes about school are not about the pompous asses of the academy but the cute asses of our childhood—about little Johnny and his teacher. Generally these are jokes about school as the scene of thinly disguised sexual repression. Why did we have to sit up straight and put our hands on our desks? What was going on below the desk?

Consider the situation: You are locked in a room, forced to sit in a row in an uncomfortable desk, and expected to write down everything a boring, often ignorant, person says. No wonder we are boring, stupid people ourselves. And no wonder almost every joke about the grammar-school classroom is about throwing the teacher on the desk and giving her the old yardstick.

But so little on the Ivory Dildo? Is it because college teachers don't inspire sexual fantasies, or is it because they want it too bad?

Did you hear the one about the professor who didn't *fuck his graduate student*?

Surely, the notorious lack of touch with reality that characterizes the college professor is fertile ground. This was the stuff of whole careers in the days of Professor Irwin Corey, a wonderful comedian who billed himself as "the world's foremost authority," and another jokester who called himself Professor Backwards.

The invasion of deadly seriousness in the form of political correctness has left the campus with a minus sense of humor. How can you make jokes in a world of feminist texts, queer theory, and honky-ology?

For those of you who don't hang in hoity-toity academic circles, here's a little etiquette advice if you ever have to attend an academic dinner party.

Lines That Won't Go Over with Academics

1. So what would you do if they phased out tenure?
2. If her faced launched a thousand ships, what did Helen of Troy's hooters do?
3. Anyone care for some dead white meat?
4. So, just what is the difference between a feminist and a bitch?
5. Did you hear about the acting professor of Polish Studies who, when denied tenure, started sending Unabomber e-mail?
6. You know we used to call it segregation until someone came up with "diversity."
7. So, who died and made you chair?

Anyone who has ever been to school has nightmares about the experience till the day he dies (being unprepared for the exam, being unable to find the classroom, being unwilling to blow the teacher). But anything that painful also has to be good for a few laughs (like marriage and death).

As a college teacher, Dobby knows what it is to cause pain. He teaches on the quarter system, and on the first day of class is met with a roomful of young, healthy, vibrant men and women. But over the weeks of the quarter, the pressures of work, party, sickness, and school take their tolls, and the students turn into sleep-deprived, caffeine-addicted zombies. When he looks out on a class at the end of the quarter and sees what used to be beautiful, healthy young people now resembling characters in a Charles Addams cartoon, he knows that education is going according to plan. He has worn down the young people, at least temporarily.

If you are currently in school, we are very sorry. If you are no longer in school ("Great God Almighty, free at last!"), never let them lock you up again.

>> SUBJECT: Academia: The Ivory Dildo

>> A guy goes in a bar and orders a beer. After a while this really gorgeous woman walks in and sits beside him. He starts thinking about talking her into going to bed with him and with a smile he turns to her, "Hi. Would you like me to buy you a drink?"

The woman turns to him and screams at the top of her lungs, "*What?* You want to *fuck me*? No way!"

Every discussion in the bar suddenly stops and all the people are staring at the guy as the woman walks away from the bar. The guy gets really embarrassed, but he sits still on his stool as if nothing has happened.

After a while the same woman walks up to him again and tells him, "I'm sorry about that little incident, but you see I'm a psychology graduate student, and I wanted to see how people react to embarrassing situations."

The guy then yells, "*What*? Two-hundred bucks for a *blow job*? No way!"

>> Little Johnny was sitting in class doing math problems when his teacher picked him to answer a question.

"Johnny, if there were five birds sitting on a fence and you shot one with your gun, how many would be left?"

"None," replied Johnny. "'Cause the rest would fly away."

"Well, the answer is four," said the teacher. "But I like the way you're thinking."

Little Johnny said, "I have a question for you now. If there were three women eating ice-cream cones in a shop, one licking her cone, the second biting her cone, and the third one sucking her cone, which one is married?"

"Well," said the teacher nervously, "I guess the one sucking the cone?"

"No," said Little Johnny. "The one with the wedding ring on her finger, but I like the way you're thinking."

» A student comes to a young professor's office hours. She glances down the hall, closes his door and kneels pleadingly. "I would do anything to pass this exam."

She leans closer to him, flips back her hair, gazes meaningfully into his eyes, "I mean," she whispers, "I would do anything...."

He returns her gaze, "Anything?"

"Anything."

His voice softens, "Anything?"

"Anything," she repeats again.

His voice turns to a whisper. "Would you ... study?"

» A young boy was in fourth grade and was having a terrible time with math. His parents worked with him night after night but there was no improvement. His math marks were dismal. Desperate, his parents decided to transfer their son to a new school. Although not religious, they checked around and found that the Catholic school seemed to have a good academic record. They enrolled their son, and immediately the boy's math scores soared. He went from a failing grade to become an A student in a matter of weeks.

His parents were surprised at the change and over dinner one night they asked their son about his improvement. "Was it better teaching?" they asked and the boy said "No, the teachers are about the same."

"Was it a different textbook?"

Again the boy said, "No, it's the same textbook"

Finally they asked their son why he thought he had made such a dramatic improvement. The boy said, "The first day I went to school I knew they took their math seriously and that I had to do well or there would be terrible consequences: The first thing I saw when I went into the classroom was some guy nailed to a plus sign."

>> Blonde one: "Have you ever read Shakespeare?"

Blonde two: "No, who wrote it?"

>> A professor of ebonics goes into the office of a professor of mathematics and says, "Hey, say something in math."

The math guy thinks and says, "πr^2"

The ebonics guy thinks and says, "No, pie are round. Cornbread are square."

>> A man in his mid-thirties decided that he wanted to go back to school, but just to take some courses that he found interesting. Unfortunately, when he went to register, he found that all the classes he had intended to take were already too full. Disappointed, the man figured, "Ah screw it."

The next day, the man happened to run into one of the professors who taught at the university. The man explained his situation to the professor, to which the professor replied, "Hey, if nothing else, why not sign up for my course in logic?"

Intrigued, the man asked the professor, "What exactly do you teach in your class?"

"Well," the professor answered, "I'll give you an example of what I mean. Do you own a weed whacker?"

"Yes," the man replied.

"If you own a weed whacker, then you probably have a lawn," the professor said.

"Yes," the man replied.

"And if you have a lawn, then you probably own a home, right?" the professor asked.

"Yes," the man replied

"And if you own a home, then you probably are married with a family, correct?" the professor asked.

"Why yes," the man replied

"And if you are married with a family, then you're in all probability heterosexual, right?" the professor asked

"Yes!" the man replied and left.

The following day, the man decided to try out some of this "logic" on the clerk at the store, because he was so impressed with it himself.

The man asks the clerk, "Do you own a weed whacker?"

"No" the clerk replies.

"Ah-hah!" the man blurts out, "You must be gay!"

>> Son: "Dad, I have to do a special report for school. Can you help me answer these questions for my homework?

Father: "Sure, Son. Ask away."

Son: "What is politics?"

Father: "Well, let's take our home for example. I am the wage earner, so let's call me 'Capitalism.' Your mother is the administrator of money, so we'll call her 'Government.' We take care of your needs, so we'll call you 'The People.' We'll call the maid 'The Working Class,' and your baby brother we can call 'The Future.' Do you understand, Son?"

Son: "I'm not really sure, Dad. I'll have to think about it."

That night, awakened by his baby brother's crying, the boy went to see what was wrong. Discovering that the baby had seriously dirtied his diaper, the boy went to his parents' room and found his mother sound asleep. So he went to the maid's room, where, peeking through the keyhole, he saw his father in bed fucking the maid. He pounded on the door, but his knocking was totally ignored by the preoccupied father and maid. So the boy returned to his room and went back to sleep.

The next morning he reported to his father: "Dad, I think I understand what politics is."

Father: "Good, son! Can you explain it to me in your own words?"

Son: "Well Dad, while Capitalism is screwing the Working Class, Government is sound asleep, the

People are being completely ignored, and the Future is full of shit."

>> PROFESSOR: Although in modern English the double negative is usually taken to mean an affirmative, in many linguistic contexts the double negative is an intensified negative, just as the double affirmative is always an intensified affirmative. Indeed, there is no known case of a double affirmative being used as a negative.

STUDENT: Yeah, right.

12

Lawyers@
workplace
.scum

WHAT CAN YOU SAY about the workplace in the nineties? Nothing out loud or someone will sue your ass. So you plop in front of a computer and type:

Ten Things I'd Rather Be Doing Right Now

1. Boffing the boss's wife
2. Boffing the boss's son
3. Stealing office supplies
4. Calling the bitch in the next chair "bitch"
5. Sticking the consultant's body in the trunk of his Lexus
6. Having a three martini lunch, like in the '50s
7. Updating my resume (but it's on my home computer)
8. Surfing the Net for erotic chat rooms
9. Finding out my stock options made me a millionaire so i can quit
10. Going postal

The computer presents a high-tech fuck-off op. Workers of the World, log on! You have nothing to lose but your productivity.

And fuck-off we must, as the pressures mount. The speedups, lack of job security, and need to climb up the downsizing ladder are not the only workplace problems. Enter the lawyer.

We have lumped some of our favorite lawyer jokes with work jokes because, if any single group has contributed to the unbearable heaviness of going to work, it's the goddamn lawyers.

Q: How have lawyers made the workplace worse?

A: Sexual-harassment suits, product-liability suits, and hideous three-piece suits.

These jokes reflect a feeling that work is hell and lawyers are on Satan's staff.

It is the frustration and angst of the workplace which has led to the computer-generated career-ender known in psychiatric circles as the Freudian Send. In this situation, you want to send a co-worker an e-mail about someone at work you think is an asshole. You are so obsessed with the objet d' e-mail that you accidentally put that person's name on the "To:" line. You hit "send" and before you know it, ka-boom:

To: Jane the Boss

From: Joe Schmo

Subject: Jane's Ass

Hey, Fred, don't you think Jane's tight skirt shows what a big fat ass she has?

One of the most famous Freudian Sends of all time involved the reporter at the *Los Angeles Times* who sent a colleague an e-mail describing what a freak the punkish son of his editor was. Unfortunately the e-mail was sent to said editor. There was speculation the reporter would be fired. But his was a strange hell: The San Francisco bureau of the *Los Angeles Times*.

Moral of the story: If you're bored at work, call your lawyer. Why screw yourself?

>> SUBJECT: Lawyers@workplace.scum

>> A doctor and a lawyer in separate vehicles collided on I-95 one foggy night. The fault was questionable, but both were shaken up. The lawyer kindly offered the doctor a drink from a pocket flask. The doctor took the flask with a shaking hand and belted back a couple of swallows. As the lawyer started to put the cap back on the flask the doctor asked, "Aren't you going to have one too, for your nerves?"

"Of course I am," replied the lawyer, "after the highway patrol gets here."

>> In a long line of people waiting for a bank teller, one guy suddenly started massaging the back of the person in front of him. Surprised, the man in front turned and snarled, "Just what the hell you are doing?"

"Well," said the guy, "you see, I'm a chiropractor, and I could see that you were tense, so I had to massage your back. Sometimes I just can't help practicing my art."

"That's the stupidest thing I've ever heard," the guy replied. "Look, I'm a lawyer. Am I fucking the guy in front of me?"

>> A man takes the day off from work and decides to go out golfing. He is on the second hole when he notices a frog sitting next to the green. He thinks

nothing of it and is about to shoot when he hears, "Ribbit. Nine iron." The man looks round and doesn't see anyone, so he tries again. "Ribbit. Nine iron." He looks at the frog and decides to prove the frog wrong, puts his other club away, and grabs a nine iron. Boom! He hits a birdie. He is shocked.

He says to the frog, "Wow! That's amazing. You must be a lucky frog, eh?"

The frog replies, "Ribbit. Lucky frog. Lucky frog."

The man decides to take the frog with him to the next hole.

"What do you think, frog?" the man asks.

"Ribbit. Three wood," was the reply. The guy takes out a three wood and boom! Hole in one. The man is befuddled and doesn't know what to say.

By the end of the day, the man had golfed the best game of golf in his life and asks the frog, "OK, where to next?"

The frog replies, "Ribbit. Las Vegas."

They go to Las Vegas, and the guy says, "OK frog, now what?"

The frog says, "Ribbit. Roulette."

Upon approaching the roulette table the man asks, "What do you think I should bet?"

The frog replies, "Ribbit. $3000. Black six." Now, it's a million to one shot that this would win, but after the golf game, the man figures what the heck. Boom! Tons of cash comes sliding back across the table.

The man takes his winnings and buys the best room in the hotel. He sits the frog down and says, "Frog, I don't know how to repay you. You won me all this money, and I am forever grateful."

The frog replies, "Ribbit. Kiss Me."

He figures why not, since after all the frog did for him, he deserves it. All of a sudden the frog turns into the most gorgeous sixteen-year-old girl in the world.

"And that, Your Honor, is how the girl ended up in my room."

>> Q: What's brown and looks good on a lawyer?

A: Shit.

>> Q: What's the difference between God and a lawyer?

A: God doesn't think he's a lawyer.

>> Q: What's the difference between a lawyer and a prostitute?

A: Clothes.

>> Q: Why should lawyers be buried 100 feet deep?

A: Because deep down, they're really good people.

>> Q: How do you save a drowning lawyer?

A: Take your foot off his head.

>> Q: How do you get a lawyer out of a tree?

A: Cut the rope.

>> Q: What do you have when a lawyer is buried up to his neck in wet cement?

A: Not enough cement.

>> Q: You're trapped in a room with a tiger, a rattlesnake and a lawyer. You have a gun with two bullets. What should you do?

A: Shoot the lawyer. Twice.

>> An old man was critically ill. Feeling that death was near, he called his lawyer. "I want to become a lawyer. How much is it for that express degree you told me about?"

"It's $50,000," the lawyer said. "But why? You'll be dead soon, why do you want to become a lawyer?"

"That's my business! Get me the course!"

Four days later, the old man got his law degree. His lawyer was at his bedside, making sure his bill would be paid.

Suddenly the old man was racked with fits of coughing, and it was clear that this would be the end. Still curious, the lawyer leaned over and said, "Please, before it's too late, tell me why you wanted to get a law degree so badly before you died?"

In a faint whisper, as he breathed his last, the old man said, "One less lawyer."

>> A man was sent to hell for his sins. As he was being taken to his place of eternal torment, he passed a room where a lawyer was having an intimate conversation with a beautiful young woman. "What a rip-off," the man muttered. "I have to roast for all eternity, and that lawyer gets to spend it with a beautiful woman."

Jabbing the man with his pitchfork, the escorting demon snarled, "Who are you to question that woman's punishment?"

>> A dedicated shop steward was at a convention in Las Vegas and decided to check out the local brothels. When he got to the first one, he asked the madam, "Is this a union house?"

"No, I'm sorry it isn't."

"Well, if I pay you one hundred dollars, what cut do the girls get?"

"The house gets eighty dollars, and the girls get twenty dollars."

Mightily offended at such unfair dealings, the man stomped off down the street in search of a more equitable shop.

His search continued for quite a while. Finally he reached a brothel where the madam said, "Why yes, this is a union house."

"And if I pay you one hundred dollars, what cut do the girls get?"

"The girls get eighty dollars, and the house gets twenty dollars."

"That's more like it!" the man said. He looked around the room and pointed to a stunningly attractive redhead. "I'd like her for the night."

"I'm sure you would, sir," said the madam, gesturing to a fat fifty-year-old woman in the corner, "but Ethel here has seniority."

» "I want to open a fuckin' checking account," the man said.

"I beg your pardon. What did you say?" the teller replied.

"Listen up damn it. I said I want to open a fuckin' checking account, right now."

"Sir, I'm sorry, but we do not tolerate that kind of language in this bank." The teller left the window and went over to the bank manager and told him the problem.

They both returned, and the manager asked, "What seems to be the problem here?"

"There's no fuckin' problem," the man said. "I just won fifty million in the lottery, and I want to open a fuckin' checking account in this fuckin' bank."

"I see sir," the manager said, "and this bitch is giving you a hard time?"

» Advice for office managers: If you keep the sexual harassment complaint forms in the bottom drawer, then you'll get a great view of the women's butts when they get one out.

>> A small business owner was faced with the problem of having to downsize his company. He added up all the receipts and discovered he had to fire one of his employees. He looked in his files and saw that his newest employees were Diane and Jack.

Because they had started on the same day at the same time, he wondered how he would make the decision on who to fire. Finally he decided that he would fire the first one he saw taking a break. About ten minutes later he saw Diane leaning against the wall next to the watercooler.

He walked over to her with a serious look on his face and said, "Diane, it seems as though I'm going to have to either lay you or Jack off."

Diane looked at her employer and said, "Well, you're going to have to jack off, because I have a headache."

13

Final
Subject:
The End

ALL OF THESE JOKES WERE E-MAILED to us in the last year, but of course many of these jokes are old jokes made new again in cyberspace. As Gershon Legman (author of the two-thousand-page, two-volume work, *The Rationale of the Dirty Joke*) has pointed out, jokes aren't invented, they evolve.

It used to take maybe a week for a joke to make its way across country (the oral tradition), but now a good joke moves around the country in seconds (the cyber tradition). This allows what goes around to come around again and again.

Jokes are the original form of literature. In the caves, cavemen told jokes about cavewomen (and vice versa) and laughed.

> *Caveman: I said to her, "Woman bring me my meat."*
> *And she said, "Beat it."*
>
> *Other Cavemen: Ha-ha.*

Of course, we no longer get it.

All jokes are divided into *tres partes*: the hook, the setup, and the punch line. Novels are like jokes with really really long setups. While we read for the setup, we like the payoff at the end—the punch line. Some jokes, like novels, have such great setups that we'll accept not-so-great punch lines. But there is a point at which, if the payoff is too lame (the horrible pun punch line) or too far away (the shaggy-dog joke), even the most fascinating setup becomes a big waste of time.

Poems are also like jokes: you gotta have a payoff.

Shall I compare thee to a summer's day?
Maybe not.

See, it wouldn't have worked without the payoff.

Old jokes come back. Many Bill Clinton jokes are variations on Ozark jokes from the late nineteenth century, jokes about doin' it with kinfolk or havin' sex with chickens. (They couldn't have foreseen Al Gore, though.)

You listen to an old joke well-told (or well e-mailed) and think: Tell it again, Sam.

If you've heard some of the preceding jokes before, think of them like old songs that are worth hearing again.

So tell or e-mail your friends these jokes or, even better, buy them their own copy of this book. (And if you come across a really good one, e-mail it to us at Cyberlaffs@aol.com).

If you stay on line long enough, every old joke you've ever heard in your life will eventually come back to you over the Net. We know the first dirty joke we heard will eventually find new life in cyberspace. We're waiting for the following e-mail:

To: Cyberlaffs@aol.com
From: Anonymous Fifth Grader
Subject: Johnny Fuckerfaster